AF474921

Atharvaśira Upaniṣat

(Śivātharva-Śīrṣam)

अथर्वशिर उपनिषत्

(शिवाथर्वशीर्षम्)

With Sanskrit Text

Vishwambhar 'Vishu' Sharma

All Rights Reserved

First Edition	....	….	….	April 2020
Second Edition	….	….	….	October 2020

Contact: SharmaBook.Publish@gmail.com

Dedicated to

Ancient Sages of India

Read Author's Other Book:

Śrĩmad Bhāgavatam: In Four Verses

Preface

Desirous of liberation, I indeed surrender to that Effulgent Being who in the beginning created Brahmā (the creator) and delivered him the Vedas, and who reveals [to sincere seekers] the divine knowledge of the Ātman (the Inner Self).

Śvetāśvatara Upaniṣad VI.18

For whom is this book?

This book is intended for the readers who are interested in Indian spirituality and would love to study the Vedic (Hindu) scriptures, especially the *Upaniṣads*. The knowledge of Sanskrit is not necessary since I have translated all the Sanskrit texts, but the reader will undoubtedly enjoy it more if he/she knows some Sanskrit.

For those who are not familiar with the transliteration of the Sanskrit alphabet, it has been explained in Appendix B.

What is this book about?

The *Atharva-Śira Upaniṣat* is one of the minor *Upaniṣads*; it certainly is not trivial in its contents since it is full of Vedantic wisdom. This *Upaniṣad* glorifies Rudra, who is identified with *Brahman*, the Ultimate Reality. Rudra is a Vedic name of Lord Śiva, and therefore, the *Atharva-Śira Upaniṣat* comes under the category of *Śaiva Upaniṣads*. Being a *Śaiva Upaniṣad*, it is also known as *Śiva-Atharva-Śīrṣam*. Other *Śaiva Upaniṣads* are *Atharvaśikhā Upaniṣad*, *Nīlarudra Upaniṣad*, *Kālāgnirudra Upaniṣad*, and *Kaivalya Upaniṣad*. The *Śvetāśvatara Upaniṣad*, which is one of the 12 major *Upaniṣads*, may also be considered as a *Śaiva Upaniṣad*. *Atharva-Śira Upaniṣat* is undoubtedly an ancient scripture, full of spiritual wisdom.

There are five *Atharva-Śīrṣas* dedicated to Hindu Deities *Gaṇeśa*, Śiva, *Viṣṇu*, Goddess *Durgā*, and *Sūrya* (Sun-god), each Deity is addressed as the Supreme Being – *Brahman* or the Ultimate Truth. This signifies the fact that there is only one God, but He has been given numerous names. The most common *Atharva-Śīrṣa* is the *Gaṇapati Atharva-Śīrṣa*, which is dedicated to Lord *Gaṇeśa*.

All the *Atharva-Śīrṣas* have an exceptional role – on the one hand, they are Vedāntic treatises in which these Deities have been identified as *Brahman*, and on the other hand, they are chanted as Vedic mantras in the praise and worship of their respective Deities. Thus, they emphasize that for God-realization, *Jñāna* (knowledge or wisdom) and *Bhakti* (devotion) must go hand in hand, they cannot be separated.

The *Atharva-Śira Upaniṣat* (*Śiva-Atharva-Śīrṣam*) has one more specialty; it not only talks about the spiritual knowledge and devotion; it also discusses spiritual practices (*sādhanā*) – meditation on various Deities – and explains which meditation will lead to attaining liberation. Among all the *Atharva-Śīrṣas*, the *Śiva-Atharva-Śīrṣam* is the longest and more detailed.

About this book

This is the revised version of the book. The first version was published in April 2020. I have made minor changes to clarify the meaning of the mantras and elaborated on some of the explanations.

The reader should note that the transliterated Sanskrit words are written in *Italic* unless they are part of the English language, e.g., Veda, Vedas, Dharma, Karma, etc. I have also not italicized the names Śiva and Rudra.

Anywhere I have used masculine words like 'he' or 'his' for a person in general or God, it is merely due to language limitations. They are meant for persons of all genders, and gods as well as goddesses, where applicable.

|| ॐ ||

Acknowledgments

[1]I express my sincere gratitude towards Mr. Prem L. Sharma of Atlanta, Georgia, for reviewing my work before its publication. From time to time, he has explained to me the significance of the mantras of the *Atharva-Śira Upaniṣat*. Mr. Prem Sharma is a retired Professional Engineer. He is a Sanskrit and Vedic scholar, a Vedantic teacher, and the author of many religious as well as philosophical books. He graciously agreed to explain the significance of the *Atharva-Śirṣas*, which is given in Appendix A.

I also express my thanks to my daughter Nisha Ward who reviewed the final manuscript.

Last but not least, I offer my sincere thanks to Madhu Sharma, my loving and charming wife of more than 53 years, for her patience and support while I was busy writing this book.

|| ॐ ||

---

[1] Only the original version of the book was reviewed by Prem Sharma, not the second edition.

Table of Contents

Introduction

Prayers

श्रीगणेशवन्दना

Śrī Gaṇeśa-Vandanā

Prayer to Lord *Śrī Gaṇeśa*

यं ब्रह्म वेदान्तविदो विदन्ति
परं प्रधानं पुरुषं तथान्ये।
विश्वोद्गतेः कारणमीश्वरं वा
तस्मै नमो विघ्नविनाशनाय॥

Yaṁ Brahma vedāntavido vidanti
Paraṁ Pradhānaṁ Puruṣaṁ tathānye |
Viśvodgateḥ kāraṇamīśvaraṁ vā
tasmai namo vighnavināśanāya ||

I bow down to [the Lord], the destroyer of obstacles, who is known by the followers of Vedānta as *Brahman* (Absolute God), by others as the Supreme, who is *Pradhāna* (the chief cause of the material nature) as well as

Puruṣa (the Inner Self of all living beings). By some, He is known as the Supreme Lord, who is the cause of the creation of the universe.

श्रीगुरुवन्दना

Śrī Guru-Vandanā

Prayer to Revered Guru

ब्रह्मानन्दं परमसुखदं केवलं ज्ञानमूर्तिं
द्वन्द्वातीतं गगनसदृशं तत्त्वमस्यादिलक्ष्यम् ।
एकं नित्यं विमलमचलं सर्वधीसाक्षिभूतं
भावातीतं त्रिगुणरहितं सद्गुरुं तं नमामि ॥

गुरुगीता

Brahmānandaṁ parama-sukhadaṁ
kevalaṁ jñāna-mūrtiṁ
Dvandvātītaṁ gagana-sadṛśaṁ
tattvamasyādi-lakṣyam |
Ekaṁ nityaṁ vimala-macalaṁ
sarvadhī-sākṣibhūtaṁ
bhāvātītaṁ triguṇa-rahitaṁ
sadguruṁ taṁ namāmi ||

Guru-Gītā

I bow to the Guru, the personification of the bliss of *Brahman* (Absolute God), who bestows the supreme joy. He is one without a second, the embodiment of divine knowledge,

> beyond duality, and [untainted and all-pervading] like the sky. He directs towards the spiritual path by explaining 'Thou are That' and other scriptural proclamations. He is unparalleled, eternal, pure, steadfast, and the witness of everything [in the changing world]. He is beyond emotions and the three modes of material nature (goodness, passion, and lethargy).

Vedas and Upaniṣads

There are four Vedas – *Ṛgveda* (ऋग्वेद), *Yajurveda* (यजुर्वेद), *Sāmaveda* (सामवेद), and *Atharvaveda* (अथर्ववेद). Each Veda is further sub-divided in four parts – *Saṁhitā* (संहिता), *Brāhmaṇas* (ब्राह्मण), *Āraṇyakas* (आरण्यक), and *Upaniṣads* (उपनिषद्).

Based on functionality, the Vedas consist of two parts: (i) the *Karma-Kāṇḍa* (कर्मकाण्ड), which includes *Saṁhitās* and *Brāhmanas*, and (ii) the *Jñāna-Kāṇḍa* (ज्ञानकाण्ड), which consists of *Āraṇyakas and Upaniṣads*. The *Karma-Kāṇḍa* is about the worship of God, which includes performing ceremonial and sacrificial activities and chanting Vedic mantras. Whereas, the *Jñāna-Kāṇḍa* deals with the knowledge of *Brahman* (ब्रह्मन्), the Ultimate Truth. The *Upaniṣads* are also known as [1]*Brahma-Vidyā* (ब्रह्मविद्या), the knowledge of *Brahman*. They are addressed as Vedānta. The word Vedānta is made up of two words, Veda + *anta*, *anta* means the end. Since the *Upaniṣads* are the last part of the Vedas, they are called Vedānta. They are the goal of the Vedas. It is also said that the *Upaniṣads* are the culmination of the Vedas.

[2]According to the book '108 *Upaniṣad[s]*, *Jñāna Kāṇḍa*' (see Bibliography), it is believed that there are 1180 branches (*Śākhās* शाखा) of the Vedas, and each branch has one *Upaniṣad*. Thus, there should be 1180 *Upaniṣads*. However, most of them are lost, and at present, we have about 250 of them available, and more than 200 have been printed.

There are about 12 major or principal *Upaniṣads*, and the rest of them are minor ones. Major *Upaniṣads* are those on which great saints and thinkers like *Ādi Śaṅkarācārya*, *Rāmānujācārya*, *Mādhvācārya*, etc., have written commentaries. When we refer to many of the *Upaniṣads* as minor, it does not mean that their contents are of less importance.

According to the *Upaniṣads*, the Supreme Being is called *Brahman*, Absolute God, or the Ultimate Reality. He has no

---

[1] The reader must note that *Brahman* or *Brahma* (ब्रह्मन् or ब्रह्म) is also referred to as the Ultimate Reality, Ultimate Truth, Absolute God, or God-Absolute. It is different from *Brahmā* (ब्रह्मा) – the creator, *Brāhmaṇa* (ब्राह्मण) – a part of Veda, or Brahmin – a priest.

[2] Scholars may differ on the actual number of the *Upaniṣads* and how many are available and printed. According to some, 280 *Upaniṣads* are available.

form or attributes and is known as *Sat-Cit-Ānanda* (सत्-चित्-आनन्द), Existence-Consciousness-Bliss. He manifests as *Īśvara* (ईश्वर), the Lord of the universe. *Īśvara* has attributes, but no form. The *Upaniṣads* emphasize the oneness of the *Ātman* (आत्मन्, the Individual Self) and *Brahman* (the Ultimate Reality or the Cosmic Self) – this is the path of knowledge or the path of non-duality.

Atharvaśīrṣas

The *Atharvaśira Upaniṣat* is also known as *Śira Upaniṣat* or *Atharva-Śīrṣam.* It glorifies the Vedic God Rudra as *Brahman*, the Ultimate Reality. Since Rudra is synonymous with Lord Śiva, this *Upaniṣad* is also called *Śivātharva-Śīrṣam*. Rudra (or Lord Śiva) is the *Ātman*, the Inner Self of all living beings; all gods (*devas*), as well as this universe, are His manifestation. He is all; nothing exists, but Him. *Śira* or *Śīrṣa* means head. *Atharvaśira* or *Atharva-śīrṣa* literally means the one whose head is *Atharva;* the word *Atharva* means 'the one who has a firm and steady mind or who is steadfast. [1] *Atharva-śīrṣa* is also one of the 1008 names of Lord Śiva given in the *Mahābhārata.*

Śiva devotees recite the *Śivātharva-Śīrṣam* during the worship of Lord Śiva. Thus, this *Upaniṣad* gives equal

---

[1] *Mahābhārata, Anuśāsana Parva*, 17.91

importance to *Jñāna* (spiritual knowledge) as well as *Bhakti* (devotion).

There are five *Atharva-Śīrṣas*:

i. *Śiva-Atharva-Śīrṣam* (शिवाथर्वशीर्षम्) – It glorifies Rudra (Lord Śiva).

ii. *Sūrya-Atharva-Śīrṣam* (सूर्याथर्वशीर्षम्) – It glorifies *Āditya* (*Sūrya*, Sun-God).

iii. *Gaṇapati-Atharva-Śīrṣam* (गणपत्यथर्वशीर्षम्) – It glorifies Lord *Gaṇeśa.*

iv. *Devī-Atharva-Śīrṣam* (देव्याथर्वशीर्षम्) – It glorifies Goddess *Durgā.*

v. *Nārāyaṇa-Atharva-Śīrṣam* (नारायणाथर्वशीर्षम्) – It glorifies Lord *Viṣṇu* (*Nārāyaṇa*).

These five Deities together are known as *Pañca-Deva* (पञ्चदेव). All these five *Atharva-Śīrṣas* are associated with the *Atharva-Veda.*

When you read these *Atharva-Śīrṣas*, you will find that the Deity of each *Atharva-Śīrṣa* is addressed as the Supreme Being, who not only creates, sustains, and annihilates the universe, but also, He/She is the one from whom the other Deities have come forth. Thus, each of the five Deities represents *Brahman*, the Ultimate Truth.

If you read the *Purāṇas*, there too, you will find a similar concept. In the [1]*Sanātana* Dharma (Hindu Dharma), there are many ways to worship – *Śaivites* worship Lord Śiva, *Vaiṣṇavas* worship Lord *Viṣṇu* (विष्णु), *Śāktas* worship Goddess *Durgā* (दुर्गा), and so on, each believing that his/her Deity is the Supreme Being. However, the basic tenets remain the same, and therefore, instead of having any conflict between these groups – fighting one another – the followers of different groups or *sampradāyas* (सम्प्रदाय), have respected and worshipped the Deities of other denominations too. All these groups together became part of one Dharma, which is known as the *Sanātana* Dharma. The beauty of the *Sanātana* Dharma is that there is only one God, but we have given Him many names and worship Him in many forms. That is what the *Ṛgveda* I.164.46 proclaims – *Ekaṁ sad viprā bahudhā vadanti* (एकं सद् विप्रा बहुधा वदन्ति), the Truth (meaning, God) is one, but the wise describe it (Him) in various ways.

All the *Atharva-Śīrṣas* serve the worship part of the Vedas because they are recited during the worship of their respective Deities, and at the same time, they teach the profound knowledge of the *Upaniṣads* because their Deities are the personification of *Brahman*, Absolute God.

Among all the five *Atharva-Śīrsās*, *Śiva-Atharva-Śīrṣa* is the longest one. It consists of six mantras, which are mainly

---

[1] *Sanātana* (सनातन) Dharma or Vedic Dharma are more appropriate terms for what is commonly referred to as the Hindu religion. *Sanātana* means eternal. In Sanskrit, the correct pronunciation of the word Vedic is *Vaidika* (वैदिक).

written in prose, praising Rudra, who is identified with *Brahman*. After the six mantras, it gives *Phala-Śruti*. The *Phala-Śruti* gives the details of good fruits that one acquires by reciting these mantras. By correctly understanding *Śivātharva-Śīrṣam* (i.e., *Atharvaśira Upaniṣat*), and by meditating upon the half *mātrā*, as explained later in the book (Mantras 5.5 to 5.10), the aspirant can realize *Brahman* and attain *mokṣa*, i.e., liberation.

By chanting any of the five *Atharva-Śīrsās* with faith (*viśvāsa* विश्वास), humility and reverence (*śraddhā* श्रद्धा), and devotion (*bhakti* भक्ति) the aspirant can fulfill all his wishes.

Book Format

The book is aimed at two kinds of readers:

- Sincere readers: The book consists of (a) the Sanskrit text of the mantras, (b) their English transliteration, (c) their meaning, and (d) their explanation. I will also be discussing some of the Sanskrit terms to clarify their meaning. This will help the spiritual seekers in learning the philosophical understanding of the mantras.
- Devotees of Lord Śiva: Since this *Upaniṣad* is a *Śaiva* scripture, many Śiva devotees chant these mantras during the worship of Lord Śiva. For such devotees, I have dedicated two sections, which give only the

Sanskrit text of the *Upaniṣad* – that will make it easy for them to recite the mantras.

(i) One section presents the Sanskrit text in *Devanāgarī*.

(ii) The other gives its English transliteration for those who cannot read the text in *Devanāgarī*.

- I have also added an Appendix explaining the significance of the *Atharva-Śīrṣas* written by Prem L. Sharma.

Conclusion

The writing of the book is my endeavor to share my understanding of the *Atharvaśira Upaniṣat* with readers who are interested in ancient Vedic (Hindu) scriptures. I hope this book will help the seekers of Truth in their spiritual journey.

Notes:

- When referring to Rudra or Lord Śiva, who is *Brahman*, Supreme God, I have used the upper case 'G' in the word 'God,' whereas for *devas* – divine celestial beings – I have used the lower case 'g,' e.g., 'god.'
- There are lots of verses (*ślokas*) in the *Liṅga Purāṇa* which are similar to the mantras given in the

Atharvaśira Upaniṣat. I have given such verses in footnotes for information only.

- Where the Sanskrit words are too long, I have added hyphens to break the words, which will help readers to read and pronounce the words correctly.
- The plural of the transliterated Sanskrit nouns is shown by adding 's' at the end for simplification; it is not the actual plural in the Sanskrit language.
- The *Upaniṣad* has only six mantras and *phala-śruti*. In the meaning portion of the mantras, just for the sake of explanation, I have divided them into various parts – 1.1, 1.2, 1.3 or 6.1, 6.2, 6.3 …, etc.
- Legend:

Liṅga	*Liṅga Purāṇa*

|| ॐ ||

Meaning

[1]*Atharvaśira Upaniṣat*
(Śivātharva-Śīrṣam)

|| शान्तिपाठः ||
|| *Śānti-Pāṭhaḥ* ||

Peace Chant

ॐ भद्रं कर्णेभिः श‍ृणुयाम देवा भद्रं पश्येमाक्षभिर्यजत्राः ।
स्थिरैरङ्गैस्तुष्टुवाꣳसस्तनूभिर् व्यशेम हि[2] देवहितं यदायुः ॥

OM bhadraṁ karṇebhiḥ śṛṇuyāma devā
bhadraṁ paśyemā-kṣabhir-yajatrāḥ |
Sthirai-raṅgais-tuṣṭuvāgun sastanubhir

---

[1]The *Atharvaśira Upaniṣat* is also known as *Śira Upaniṣat, Atharva-Śīrṣam*, or *Śivātharva-Śīrṣam.* When it is recited in praise of Lord Śiva [in Śiva worship], it is commonly called *Śivātharva-Śīrṣam.* The Sanskrit text of this book is mainly based on *Āhnika-Sūtrāvaliḥ* (see Bibliography).

[2] In *Kṛṣṇa Yajurveda*, after *vyaśema*, there is no हि; हि means indeed.

vyaśema hi[1] *devahitaṁ yadāyuḥ* ||

OM. O gods, may we, worthy of worshipping [You], hear with our ears and see with our eyes what is auspicious. Singing songs of your praise, may we indeed live our full span of life with our sturdy limbs and bodies.

ॐ स्वस्ति [2]नऽइन्द्रो वृद्धश्रवाः स्वस्ति नः पूषा विश्ववेदाः ।
स्वस्ति नस्तार्क्ष्यो अरिष्टनेमिः स्वस्ति नो बृहस्पतिर् दधातु ॥

Om svasti [3]*na'Indro vṛddha-śravāḥ*
svasti naḥ Pūṣā viśva-vedāḥ |
Svasti nasTārkṣyo ariṣṭa-nemiḥ
svasti no Bṛhas-patir dadhātu ||

May glorious *Indra*, all-knowing *Pūṣan* (Sun-god), destroyer of evils *Tārkṣya* (celestial bird – *Garuḍa*, Lord *Viṣṇu's* vehicle), and *Bṛhaspati* (the Lord of intelligence, the guru of gods) bestow on us their blessings!

Another Sanskrit word for *svasti* (स्वस्ति) is *kalyāṇa* (कल्याण). Commonly, both words are translated as prosperity, fortune, success, or luck; however, there is no exact English word for them. *Svasti* and *kalyāṇa* both mean worldly wealth as well as spiritual good, which is the ultimate goal of the aspirant. Since

---

[1] In *Kṛṣṇa Yajurveda*, after *vyaśema*, there is no '*hi*'; '*hi*' means indeed.

[2] Alternative text: न इन्द्रो

[3] Alternative text: *na Indro*

blessing can be given for both, I have translated *svasti* as blessings.

Puṣan literally means the one who nourishes.

ॐ सह नाववतु । सह नौ भुनक्तु । सह वीर्यङ्करवावहै । तेजस्वि नावधीतमस्तु मा विद्विषावहै ॥

॥ ॐ शान्तिः शान्तिः शान्तिः ॥

Om Saha nāvavatu | Saha nau bhunaktu | Saha vīryaṅ-karavā-vahai | Tejasvi nā-vadhītamastu mā vidviṣā-vahai ||

|| *Om Śāntiḥ Śāntiḥ Śāntiḥ* ||

> May He (*Brahman* – God) protect us both [the guru and the disciple], may He nourish us both, may we both work together with tremendous strength, may our study [of scriptures] be vibrant, may we not hate each other.
>
> Peace, peace, peace!

This prayer (*Saha nāvavau …*) is chanted before and after the study or recitation of the Vedas and the *Upaniṣads*.

It is a common practice to chant the peace prayer '*Śānti*' three times to eradicate three kinds of sufferings: (i) *ādhyātmika* (आध्यात्मिक) – those caused by the own body and mind, (ii) *ādhibhautika* (आधिभौतिक) – those caused by other objects and living entities, and (iii) *ādhidaivika* (आधिदैविक) – those caused by gods or nature.

|| शिवाथर्वशीर्षम् ||

Śivātharva- Śīrṣam

अथ शिवाथर्वशीर्षम् || (अथ शिर उपनिषत्) ||

Atha Śivātharva-Śīrṣam || (Atha Śira Upaniṣat) ||

Now we begin with *Śivātharva-Śīrṣam*, also known as *Śira Upaniṣat.*

Mantra 1

Before we discuss Mantra 1, let us see how the universe was created. The *Upaniṣad*s say – in the beginning, before the manifestation of the world, *Brahman* willed, "I am one, may I become many (*Eko'haṁ bahu syām*, एकोऽहं बहु स्याम्)." The *Chāndogya Upaniṣad* (छान्दोग्य उपनिषद् 6-2-3) says – That Being (meaning *Brahman*) willed, "May I become many and grow forth." The *Aitareya Upaniṣad* (ऐतरेय उपनिषद् 1-1) says, "In the beginning, indeed, all this was *Ātman* (i.e., *Brahman*) alone. There was nothing else existing that rivaled." It further says – He willed, "Let me create the worlds."

Thus, it is *Brahman* (Absolute God), who created the world; or we may say that this world is *Brahman's* manifestation.

But, 'Who is *Brahman*?' The *Muṇḍaka Upaniṣad* (मुण्डक उपनिषद् I-1-6) describes *Brahman* as: "One who cannot be seen or grabbed; one who has no origin, color, eyes, ears, hands, or feet; one who is eternal, the lord of all, all-pervading and very subtle – the wise perceive that imperishable one as the source of all creation." It shows that *Brahman* has no form or shape (*Nirākāra* - निराकार), He is without any attributes (*Nirguṇa* - निर्गुण), and He is eternal, Meaning, He was, He is, and He will ever remain.

According to the *Chāndogya Upaniṣad* III.14.1, "All this (i.e., universe) is indeed *Brahman* (*Sarvaṁ khalvidaṁ Brahma* - सर्वं खल्विदं ब्रह्म)." It means nothing exists, but *Brahman.*

In the mid-sixties in India, I knew an old Sindhi lady whose only prayer mantra was: You alone, You alone (in the Sindhi language: *toon heen toon*, *toon heen toon* - तूं हीं तूं, तूं हीं तूं). At that time, I knew that she was praying God, but I did not know the significance of the prayer. Now, decades later, I can understand what those words meant. God alone exists – nothing exists but God. She did not pray in front of any image (*mūrti* - मूर्ति) of any Deity; it means that she was praying God having no form or shape (*Nirākāra* - निराकार). Since she only said, "You alone, You alone" and there was no "I," it meant, 'One, not two;" That is called non-duality or *Advaitavāda* (अद्वैतवाद), meaning there is no second. This is the *Advaita*-Vedānta. When there is no "I," only "Him," it is the complete surrender or the complete identification with *Brahman*; there is no 'I' or 'I-ness,' or 'Mine' or 'My-ness,' it is only *Brahman* (ब्रह्मन्), the Highest Truth.

Now, let us see what Mantra 1 talks about. It begins with a question by gods (*devas* or celestial beings) asking Rudra who He is. The summary of Rudra's reply is that He alone exists, every object in the universe is His manifestation. Thus, Rudra is another name of *Brahman.*

1.1 [1]ॐ देवा ह वै स्वर्गलोकमायंस्ते रुद्रमपृच्छन् को भवानिति ।

Om devā ha vai svarga-loka-māyaṁste rudra-mapṛcchan ko bhavāniti |

> OM. Once, the gods (*devas*) went to the blissful abode [of Rudra] and asked Him who He was.

As we know, Rudra is a Vedic name of Lord Śiva, and therefore, the words Rudra and Śiva are interchangeable. Since Rudra is another name of *Brahman*, Rudra, Śiva, and *Brahman* – all three names are synonymous. *Brahman* – the Ultimate Reality or the Ultimate Truth – who is formless and attribute-less, is personified as Rudra by the seer (*Ṛṣi* - ऋषि) of the *Upaniṣad* to make it easier for the seeker of the Truth to meditate upon Him. Similarly, anywhere I am using the word Śiva, it refers to *Brahman.*

---

[1] देवा ह्यपृच्छंस्तं देवं को भवानिति शङ्करम् ॥ Liṅga II.17.9
Devā hyapṛcchaṁstaṁ devaṁ ko bhavāniti Śaṅkaram ||

I would like to point out one thing: nowhere in the *Upaniṣad*, the word Śiva is mentioned. However, since this *Upaniṣad* is also called *Śivātharva-Śīrṣam*, I will also be explaining it from the viewpoint of Śiva devotees.

Why is He called Rudra? *Ru* (रु) means fear (*bhaya* भय), and *dru* (द्रु) means to melt or to dissolve. The one who dissolves or destroys fear is called Rudra – *Ruṁ drāvayati iti Rudraḥ*. Both phrases – *Ruṁ drāvayati* (रुं द्रावयति) and *bhayaṁ nāśayati* (भयं नाशयति) – have the same meaning.

Rud also means to cry. Those who have turned away from the Self, the Divinity within, He makes them cry – *Rodayati ātma-vimukhāni iti Rudraḥ* (रोदयति आत्मविमुखानि इति रुद्रः).

Why is He called Śiva? He is called Śiva because the world rests in Him – *Śete jagat asmin iti Śivaḥ* (शेते जगत् अस्मिन् इति शिवः).

Lord Śiva is also called *Śaṅkara*. *Śaṁ* means Bliss. He is called *Śaṅkara* because He bestows Bliss upon His seekers – *Śaṁ karoti it Śaṅkaraḥ* (शं करोति इति शङ्करः).

The word Śiva also means auspicious or Blissful.

I love to give examples from the *Purāṇas* because, in the *Purāṇas*, the complex philosophies of the *Upaniṣads* are simplified and explained through stories for a common man. According to the *Purāṇas*, Lord Śiva lives in the *Śiva-Loka* (शिवलोक), the abode of Lord Śiva, also known as *Kailāsa* (कैलास). The *Śiva-Loka*, the abode of Lord Śiva or Rudra, is a blissful place, and therefore, I have translated the word *Svarga* as the blissful abode, not heaven. The *Svarga*, meaning heaven, is the place where *devas* (gods, celestial beings) live.

According to the *Śiva-Mahāpurāṇa*, *Umā-Saṁhitā* (शिवमहापुराण, उमासंहिता), Chapter 19 and *Skanda Purāṇa*, *Kāśī-Khaṇḍa* I (स्कन्दपुराण, काशीखण्ड १), Chapter 23, the *Śiva-Loka*, the abode of Lord Siva, is the highest place; nothing is more elevated than *Śiva-Loka*. One should note that this description of *Śiva-Loka*, in this context, is only symbolic; whether you call Him Rudra or Śiva, He is transcendental and all-pervading. For the sake of the seekers of the Truth, *Brahman* is personified as Rudra. He does not need an abode to live; He is all-pervading. What it means is that the seeker needs tremendous efforts, painstaking spiritual practice (*sādhanā* - साधना), and severe penance (*tapa* - तप) to seek Lord Śiva, or in other words, to realize *Brahman*.

Just a small note. Here we are talking about Lord Śiva being the Supreme Truth, and therefore, *Śiva-Loka* is described as the highest place. If you read *Vaiṣṇava Purāṇas*, they will say that the abode of Lord *Viṣṇu* is the most elevated. A sincere seeker must not get entangled whether Śiva is Supreme or it is *Viṣṇu*. Śiva and *Viṣṇu* are the names of the same Reality, the same Truth.

Quoting from the *Skanda Purāṇa* (*Kāśī-Khaṇḍa* I, Chapter 23), it is Śiva's play that He, who is *Para-Brahman* (Supreme Reality) and has no shape or form, takes a form. He is the ruler of all, and there is no one superior to Him. He creates the world, sustains it, and then devours it. He is eternal, all-pervading, and unparalleled. No one knows Him, only He knows Himself; He is the Supreme light and dwells in all hearts.

Śrīmad Bhagavad Gītā 18.61 says:

ईश्वरः सर्वभूतानां हृद्देशेऽर्जुन तिष्ठति ।

Īśvaraḥ sarva-bhūtānāṁ hṛdeśe'rjun tiṣṭhati |

Hey Arjuna, God lives in the hearts of all living beings.

Thus, the *Skanda Purāṇa* and the *Bhagavad Gītā* are referring to the same Reality who dwells within all living beings. Please note, God dwells within all living beings, including animals, birds, worms, etc.

1.2 [1]सोऽब्रवीदहमेकः [2]प्रथममासोद्वर्तामि च भविष्यामि च नान्यः कश्चिन्मत्तो व्यतिरिक्त इति ।

---

[1]अब्रवीद् भगवान् रुद्रो ह्यहमेकः पुरातनः ।
आसं प्रथम एवाहं वर्तामि च सुरोत्तमाः ॥ Liṅga II .17.10
Abravīd bhagavān Rudro hyahamekaḥ purātanaḥ |
Āsaṁ prathama evāhaṁ vartāmi ca surottamāḥ ||

भविष्यामि च लोकेऽस्मिन् मत्तो नान्यः कुतश्चन ।
व्यतिरिक्तं न मत्तोऽस्ति नान्यत् किञ्चित् सुरोत्तमाः ॥ Liṅga II.17.11
Bhaviṣyāmi ca loke'smin matto nānyaḥ kutaścana |
vyatiriktaṁ na matto'sti nānyat kiñcit surottamāḥ ||

[2] Alternative texts: प्रथममास वर्तामि or प्रथममासं वर्तामि

So'bravīdaha-mekaḥ [1]*prathama-māsod-vartāmi ca bhaviṣyāmi ca nānyaḥ kaścin-matto vyatirikta iti* |

> He (i.e., Lord Rudra) replied, "I alone exist; I was in the beginning [before the creation], I exist now [and this universe of multi-forms is my manifestation], and I will exist in the future [after the dissolution of the world]; no one [and nothing] is separate from Me."

Ahamekaḥ – *Ahaṁ ekaḥ* means I am one, meaning I alone exist. Nothing exists, but *Brahman*; all this universe is His manifestation.

Prathamamāsa[m] – It means I was the first one. Before the creation, it was only *Brahman* who existed. Nothing existed before Him, and He was always there; He is eternal.

Udvartāmi – Then He says, '*udvartāmi*' = *ud* + *vartāmi*. *Vartāmi* means 'I exist,' and *udvartāmi* means 'I burst open' or 'I go asunder.' I have translated *udvartāmi* as 'I exist now' to simplify the meaning and show that Rudra is always present.

Rudra is not different from *Brahman*. Before the manifestation of this universe, *Brahman* existed in his form-less and attribute-less state. According to the *Śruti* (Vedas or *Upaniṣads*), *Brahman* thought, 'I am one, may I be many,' and then he appeared as this manifested universe. This *Upaniṣad* gives a similar idea; Rudra says, 'I burst open,' or

---

[1] Alternative texts: *Prathama-māsa vartāmi* or *Prathama-māsṁ vartāmi*

'I go asunder.' Formless Rudra takes the form of all these galaxies, stars, planets, etc., that you see in the universe; there may be many other universes too. Of course, Rudra does not go asunder physically; He manifests as this universe consisting of all the celestial objects and energies. It is just like the scientific theory of Big Bang, according to which, before the creation, the whole universe was compressed in one dot, then there was an explosion, and suddenly this ever-expanding universe was formed.

Interestingly, a similar quote is given by Lord *Śrī Viṣṇu* in the *Bhāgavata Mahāpurāṇa* for Himself:

अहमेवासमेवाग्रे नान्यद् यत् सदसत् परम्।
पश्चादहं यदेतच्च योऽवशिष्येत सोऽस्म्यहम्॥

Ahamevā-samevāgre nānyad yat sadasat param |
Paścādahaṁ yadetacca yo'vaśiṣyeta so'smyaham ||

II.9.32

[1]In the beginning, before the manifestation of this universe, indeed, only I existed. Besides Me, nothing existed, neither anything perceptible nor imperceptible, nor was there even primordial nature, which is the cause of both perceptible and imperceptible. It is only I who exists as this manifested universe. At the

[1]The meaning is taken from the author's book *Śrīmad-Bhāgavatam*: In Four Verses; see Bibliography.

> time of the dissolution of the universe, again, it will be I who alone will remain.

It shows that Rudra or Śiva and *Viṣṇu* are the names of the same Reality. It is one God, *Śaivites* (worshippers of Lord Śiva) call Him Śiva and *Vaiṣṇavas* (worshippers of Lord *Viṣṇu*) address Him as *Viṣṇu*. *Skanda Purāṇa, Kāśī Khaṇḍa* I (स्कन्दपुराण, काशीखण्ड १), Chapter 23, Verse 41 says,

यथा शिवस्तथा विष्णुर्यथा विष्णुस्तथा शिवः ।
अन्तरं शिवविष्णोश्च मनागपि न विद्यते ॥

Yathā Śivas-tathā Viṣṇur-yathā Viṣṇus-tathā Śivaḥ |
Antaraṁ Śiva-Viṣṇośca manāgapi na vidyate ||

> As is Śiva, so is *Viṣṇu*; as is *Viṣṇu*, so is Śiva. Not even an iota of difference exists between Śiva and *Viṣṇu*.

Brahman, the Ultimate Reality, is the material and efficient cause of the world. In fact, all this universe is a manifestation of *Brahman*: *Sarvaṁ khalvidaṁ Brahma* – all this (universe) is *Brahman*. Lord Śiva and Lord *Viṣṇu* are personifications of *Brahman*, who is *Nirākāra* (having no form or shape) and *Nirguṇa* (having no attributes).

1.3a सोऽन्तरादन्तरं प्राविशद्-दिशश्चान्तरं प्राविशत् –

So'ntarā-dantaraṁ prāviśad-diśaś-cāntaraṁ prāviśat –

> He (*Brahman*) entered [and pervaded] the innermost, hidden places and all the quarters.

Here, Rudra is referring to himself in the third person. Rudra is saying that He pervades all the space in the cosmos.

Antarā-dantaraṁ prāviśad – *antarāt antaraṁ prāviśat*: *Antar* means in, inside, or within. *Antarāt antaram* means inside of the inside or within inside, and *prāviśat* means entered. I have translated the phrase as 'entered [and pervaded] the innermost, hidden places.'

Diśaḥ – It means in directions or quarters or allover.

According to science, the universe consists of billions of galaxies, each galaxy consisting of billions of stars; stars are made up of burning gases just like our sun; planets are orbiting around stars, there are black holes, dark matter, dark energy, and so on. All these came from Rudra (Śiva), but they all are inanimate (*jaḍa* जड). Then, He entered all of them as Consciousness (*chetana-tattva* चेतनतत्त्व). Thus, Consciousness is all-pervading. It is the Consciousness that creates energy; it is the energy generated by the Consciousness that makes all these celestial objects move, keeps them in balance, and makes the universe expand. In brief, Rudra, meaning *Brahman*, is the efficient (*nimitta* निमित्त) as well as the material (*upādāna* उपादान) cause of the world. Scientists believe that animate life is created from inanimate chemicals. An inanimate substance cannot produce living things. It is the all-pervading Consciousness that enters those chemicals at the right time and under right circumstances to form life.

When we call an object inanimate, is it really stationery? Not really; the electrons of each atom of that object keep continuously moving. It is the nature of electrons to keep moving. It is the play of Śiva's *Śakti* (i.e. energy), which keeps them continually in motion.

Just a small note: When we say Śiva is *Brahman*, then *Shakti* is the Consciousness. We generally translate *Shakti* as energy. But the English word energy is only the power aspect of *Shakti*. *Shakti* is live, *Shakti* is all-knowing, *Shakti* thinks, *Shakti* creates, *Shakti* is always there either in a subtle form or in an unsubtle form. Whereas you need something to create energy; energy is not independent.

In Sanskrit, the universe is called *brahmāṇḍa* (ब्रह्माण्ड): *Brahma* + *aṇḍa*, meaning *aṇḍa* (the egg) of *Brahman*, signifying that *Brahman* is the creator of the world. The root word of *Brahman* is *bṛh* (बृह्), which means to increase, to expand, or to become big; thus, *Brahman* means the one who expands. Per science, the universe is ever-expanding; the Vedic (Hindu) scriptures give the same idea – It is *Brahman* who manifests as the expanding universe.

1.3b [1]सोऽहं नित्यानित्यो व्यक्ताव्यक्तो ब्रह्माब्रह्माहं –

---

[1]नित्योऽनित्योऽहमनघो ब्रह्माहं ब्रह्मणस्पतिः। Liṅga II.17.12
Nityo'nityo'hamanagho Brahmāhaṁ brahmaṇaspatiḥ |

So'haṁ nityā-nityo vyaktā-vyakto Brahmā-Brahmāhaṁ –

> [Lord Rudra continued] – "I am That (*Brahman* who entered the whole cosmos); I am eternal as well as transitory; I am manifest as well as un-manifest; I am *Brahman* (the Absolute Reality) and as well as that which is not *Brahman*."

The universe is called *vyakta* (manifest - व्यक्त), and the primordial nature (*mūla-prakṛti* - मूलप्रकृति) is called *avyakta* (un-manifest – अव्यक्त). The primordial nature is the material cause (*upādāna* - उपादान) of the universe, whereas *Brahman* the efficient cause (*nimitta* - निमित्त). In fact, *Brahman* is also the material cause because it is He who is the cause of the primordial nature.

What does it mean by material and efficient causes? Our scriptures give an example of a pot-maker who makes a pot out of clay. The clay is the material cause of the pot, whereas the pot-maker is the efficient cause. *Brahman* is the material as well as the efficient cause of the universe.

1.3c [1]प्राञ्चः प्रत्यञ्चोऽहं दक्षिणाञ्च उदञ्चोऽह-मधश्चोर्ध्वश्चाहं दिशश्च प्रतिदिशश्चाहं –

---

[1]दिशश्च विदिशश्चाहं प्रकृतिश्च पुमानहम् ॥ Liṅga II.17.12
Diśaśca vidiśaścāhaṁ prakṛtiśca pumānaham ||

Prāñcaḥ pratyañco'haṁ dakṣiṇāñca udañco'ha-madhaś-cordhvaś-cāhaṁ diśaśca prati-diśaś-cāhaṁ –

> I am eastern, western, southern, and northern [regions]; I am above and below; I am [all] quarters (i.e., directions), including the intermediary ones.

It means that *Brahman* is omnipresent; there is no place without Him.

1.3d पुमानपुमान् स्त्रियश्चाहं सावित्र्यहं गायत्र्यहं –

Pumāna-pumān striyaś-cāhaṁ Sāvitryahaṁ Gāyatryahaṁ –

> I am a man; I am no man; I am women; I am [Goddesses] *Sāvitrī* and *Gāyatrī*.

Brahman has no gender. He is masculine, He is neuter, and He is feminine. All gods (*devatās*, i.e., divine celestial beings) and goddesses are His manifestations.

Pumānapumān – Pumān-apumān: It means man and no man. It may also be translated as *Puruṣa* (पुरुष) and *Prakṛti* (प्रकृति) instead of 'man' and 'no man' (or neuter). *Puruṣa* is *Ātman*, the Supreme Consciousness, and *Prakṛti* is the nature. The world is made up of *Puruṣa* as well as *Prakṛti.*

Śvetāśvatara Upaniṣad (श्वेताश्वतर उपनिषद्) V.10 has a similar text:

नैव स्त्री न पुमानेष न चैवायं नपुंसकः ।
यद्यच्छरीरमादत्ते तेन तेन स युज्यते ॥

Naiva strī na pumāneṣa na caivāyaṁ napunsakaḥ |
Yadyac-charīra-mādatte tena tena sa yujyte ||

He is neither female, nor male, nor neuter. He is identified with whatever body He takes.

1.3e [1]त्रिष्टुब्जगत्यनुष्टुप् चाऽहं छन्दोऽहं सत्योऽहं गार्हपत्यो दक्षिणाग्निराहवनीयोऽहं –

Triṣṭub-jagatya-nuṣṭup cā'haṁ chando'haṁ satyo'-haṁ gārhapatyo dakṣiṇāgnirāha-vanīyo'haṁ –

I am the *triṣṭubh,* the *jagatī*, and the *anuṣṭubh*; I am the meter; I am the Truth; I am *gārhapatya*, *dakṣina*, and *āhavanīya* fires.

The *Triṣṭubh*, *jagatī,* and *anuṣṭubh* are some of the meters (*chandas*) used in Sanskrit poetry.

Sanskrit poetry follows very complex rules. Generally, each verse is divided into four quarters or feet (*pādas* पाद). Each quarter has a fixed number of syllables. Each quarter, in addition to having a set number of syllables, may follow the

---

[1]त्रिष्टुब्जगत्यनुष्टुप् च च्छन्दोहं तन्मयः शिवः ।
सत्योहं सर्वगः शान्तस्त्रेताग्निर्गौरवं गुरुः ॥
Liṅga II.17.13
Triṣṭub-jagatya-nuṣṭup ca cchandohaṁ tanmayaḥ Śivaḥ |
Satyo'haṁ sarvagaḥ śāntas-tretāgnir-gauravaṁ guruḥ ||

same sequence of long (*dīrgha* दीर्घ) and short (*hrasva* ह्रस्व) syllabic instants (*mātrās*). The *Triṣṭubh*, *jagatī*, and *anuṣṭubh* meters respectively have 11, 12, and 8 syllables in each quarter, meaning 44, 48, and 32 syllables in each verse. There are many other meters too.

Gārhapatya, *dakṣina*, and *āhavanīya* are names of the holy fire used for performing a *yajña* (यज्ञ) or fire sacrifice. Together, these three fires – *gārhapatya*, *dakṣināgni*, and *āhavanīya* – are known as *tretāgni*.

1.3f [1]गौरहं गौर्यहमृगहं यजुरहं सामाहमथर्वाङ्गिरसोऽहं – *Gauraham gauryaha-mṛgaham yajuraham sāmāha-matharvāṅgi-raso'ham* –

> I am the cow; I am the female buffalo; I am *Ṛgveda*, *Yajurveda*, *Sāmaveda*, and *Atharvaveda*; I am *Aṅgirasa*.

The four Vedas, the most ancient scriptures of the *Sanātana* Dharma, i.e., Hindu Dharma, were revealed to sages during their meditation. The Vedas are the word of Rudra; He is the one who revealed them.

---

[1]गौरहं गह्वरश्चाहं नित्यं गहनगोचरः । Liṅga II.17.14
Gauraham gahvaraś-cāham nityam gahana-gocaraḥ |

ऋग्वेदोहं यजुर्वेदः सामवेदोहमात्मभूः ॥ Liṅga II.17.15
Ṛgvedoham yajurvedaḥ sāmavedoha-mātmabhūḥ ||

अथर्वणोहं मंत्रोहं तथा चांगिरसां वरः । Liṅga II.17.16
Atharvaṇoham mantroham tathā cāṅgirasām varaḥ |

यो ब्रह्माणं विदधाति पूर्वं यो वै वेदांश्च प्रह्णोति तस्मै ।

Yo Brahmāṇaṁ vidadhāti pūrvaṁ
yo vai Vedāṁśca prahṇoti tasmai |
Śvetāśvatara Upaniṣad VI.18

He (Rudra), in the beginning, created *Brahmā* (the creator) and delivered him the Vedas.

The Vedas represent Rudra, meaning *Brahman*; they are not different from Him.

Aṅgīrasa is one of the ancient sages.

1.3g [1]ज्येष्ठोऽहं श्रेष्ठोऽहं वरिष्ठोऽहमापोऽहं तेजोऽहं गुह्योऽहमरण्योऽहमक्षरमहं क्षरमहं पुष्करमहं –

Jyeṣṭho'haṁ śreṣṭho'haṁ variṣṭho'ha-māpo'haṁ tejo'haṁ guhyo'ha-maraṇyo'ha-makṣara-mahaṁ kṣaramahaṁ puṣkara-mahaṁ –

I am the eldest, the best, and superior; I am the water; I am brightness; I am the secret; I am the

---

[1]ज्येष्ठोहं सर्वतत्त्वानां वरिष्ठोहमपां पतिः । Liṅga II.17.14
Jyeṣṭhohaṁ sarva-tattvānaṁ variṣṭhoha-mapāṁ patiḥ |

अक्षरं च क्षरं चाहम् – Liṅga II.17.17
Akṣaraṁ ca kṣaraṁ cāham –

पुष्करं च पवित्रं च मध्यं चाहं ततः परम् । Liṅga II.17.18
Puṣkaraṁ ca pavitraṁ ca madhyaṁ cāhaṁ tataḥ param |

forest; I am imperishable as well as perishable;
I am *Puṣkara*.

Puṣkara – It is the name of one of the most famous and significant ancient pilgrimage places for the followers of the *Sanātana* Dharma. It is located near Ajmer in Rajasthan, India. It is considered as the king of all pilgrimage places. Here, *Puṣkara* is identified with Lord Rudra.

In *Puṣkara*, there is a temple of Lord *Brahmā*, the creator. This temple is believed to be more than 2000 years old. *Brahmā's* temples are very, very rare; there are only a few. When Lord Rudra says, 'I am *Puṣkara*,' what He means is that He is *Brahmā*, the creator. *Puṣkara* also means 'blue lotus flower.' A lotus flower grows in mud but always stays above its surface, and therefore it does not get dirty. A person, who is unattached to the world, and remains unperturbed by the ups and downs and pleasures and pains in life, is compared with the lotus flower. Thus, Lord Rudra says that, though he pervades the whole world, He is unaffected by its limitations.

1.3h [1]पवित्रमहमुग्रञ्च [2]बलिश्च पुरस्ताज्ज्योतिरित्यहमेव सर्वेभ्यो मामेव स सर्वः [3]समो यो मां वेद स देवान्वेद सर्वांश्च वेदान् साङ्गानपि –

Pavitra-maha-mugrañca [4]baliśca purastāj-jyotiritya-hameva sarvebhyo māmeva sa sarvaḥ [5]samo yo māṁ veda sa devān-veda sarvāṁśca vedān sāṅgānapi –

> I am pure but also fierce; I am the sacrifice; I am at the beginning; I indeed am the light [that illumines all]; [I am] for all; to Me, all are the same (meaning, I do not discriminate). One who knows Me thus knows all the gods (*devas*) and the Vedas, including the Limbs of Vedas.

There are four Vedas – *Ṛgveda*, *Yajurveda*, *Sāmaveda*, and *Atharvaveda.* Also, there are six 'Limbs of Vedas,' known as

---

[1]ज्योतिश्चाहं तमश्चाहं ब्रह्माविष्णुमहेश्वरः । Liṅga II.17.19
Jyotiṣ-cāhaṁ tamaś-cāhaṁ Brahmā-Viṣṇu-Maheśvaraḥ |

एवं सर्वं च मामेव यो वेद सुरसत्तमाः ।
स एव सर्ववित् सर्वं सर्वात्मा परमेश्वरः ॥ Liṅga II.17.20
Evaṁ sarvaṁ ca māmeva yo veda sura-sattamāḥ |
Sa eva sarvavit sarvaṁ sarvamātmā parameśvaraḥ ||

[2]Alternative text: बहिश्च.

[3]Alternative texts: समायो or स मां यो.

[4] Alternative text: *bahiśca.*

[5] Alternative texts: *samāyo* or *sa māṁ yo.*

Vedāṅgas (वेदाङ्ग). The word *Vedāṅga* is made up two words Veda (वेद) + *Aṅga* (अङ्ग); *aṅga* means limb, limbs of the Vedas. They are – *Śikṣā* (शिक्षा - proper pronunciation), *Chandas* (छन्द - prosody or poetic meters), *Vyākaraṇa* (व्याकरण - grammar), *Nirukta* (निरुक्त - etymology), *Kalpa* (कल्प - instruction for how to perform Vedic rites or worship), and *Jyotiṣa* (ज्योतिष - astronomy and astrology). The study of these subjects is part of learning Vedas.

1.3i [1]ब्रह्म ब्राह्मणैश्च गां गोभिर्-ब्राह्मणान् ब्राह्मणेन हविर्हविषा आयुरायुषा सत्यं सत्येन धर्मेण धर्मं तर्पयामि स्वेन तेजसा ।

Brahma brāhmaṇaiśca gāṁ gobhir - brāhmaṇān brāhmaṇena havir-haviṣā āyurāyuṣā satyaṁ satyen dharmeṇa dharmaṁ tarpayāmi svena tejasā |

> With my splendor, I satisfy *Brahman* (Absolute God) through Brahmins (priests or pious people), cow through cows, Brahmins through Brahmins, oblation through oblation,

---

[1]गां गोभिर्ब्राह्मणान् सर्वान् ब्राहमण्येन हवींषि च ।
आयुषायुस्तथा सत्यं सत्येन सुरसत्तमाः ॥ Linga II.17.21
Gāṁ gobhir brāhmaṇān sarvān brāhmaṇyena havīṁṣi ca |
Āyuṣāyus-tathā satyaṁ satyena sura-sattamāḥ ||

धर्मं धर्मेण सर्वांश्च तर्पयामि स्वतेजसा । Linga II.17.22
Darmaṁ dharmeṇa sarvāṁśca tarpayāmi svatejasā |

> life through life, Truth through Truth, Dharma through Dharma.

This is very interesting; Rudra says that He satisfies *Brahman* (the Ultimate Reality) through Brahmins (pious people or priestly class). Earlier it was noted that there is no difference between Rudra and *Brahman*, it means that Rudra pleases Himself through Brahmins. How? Due to Lord Rudra's grace, Brahmins are full of faith and reverence for *Brahman*, and thus because of their austerity and truthful nature, they please *Brahman* or Rudra.

Who is a Brahmin? According to *Śrīmad Bhagavad Gītā* 18.42:

शमो दमस्तपः शौचं क्षान्तिरार्जवमेव च ।
ज्ञानं विज्ञानमास्तिक्यं ब्रह्मकर्म स्वभावजम् ॥

Śamo damas-tapaḥ śaucaṁ kṣānti-rārjavameva ca |
Jñānaṁ vijñāna-māstikyaṁ brahma-karma svabhāvjam ||

> Control of the mind and senses, austerity, [external as well as internal] purity, forgiveness, straightforwardness, faith in the Vedas, spiritual knowledge, Self-realization – these are the natural actions of a Brahmin.

It is also said: One who knows *Brahman* is a Brahmin – *Brahma jānāti brāhmaṇaḥ* (ब्रह्म जानाति ब्राह्मणः).

With Lord Rudra's grace, the species of cows are protected through progeny, and Brahmins are protected by themselves through their austerity and by sharing their wisdom and knowledge with others.

Havi means 'oblation' or any material offered to gods by putting it in the holy fire (*homam* or *havan* or *yajña* or sacred fire). When *havi* is offered, gods in return grant prosperity and good life to worshippers so that they can provide more oblations to gods. Thus, the cycle goes on. Lord *Kṛṣṇa* says in the *Bhagavad-Gītā* III.10-11:

सहयज्ञाः प्रजाः सृष्ट्वा पुरोवाच प्रजापतिः ।
अनेन प्रसविष्यध्वमेष वोऽस्त्विष्टकामधुक् ॥
देवान्भावयतानेन ते देवा भावयन्तु वः ।
परस्परं भावयन्तः श्रेयः परमवाप्स्यथ ॥

Sahayajñāḥ prajāḥ sṛṣṭvā purovāca Prajāpatiḥ |
Anena prasaviṣyadhva - meṣa vo'stviṣṭa - kāmadhuk ||
Devān - bhāvayatānena te devā bhāvayantu vaḥ |
Parasparaṁ bhāvayantaḥ śreyaḥ parama-vāpsyatha ||

> In the beginning, having created mankind along with *yajña* (the sacrifice, or the spirit of charity), *Brahmā* (the Creator) said [to people], "By this (*yajña*) shall you prosper; may this fulfill your desires. Please the gods with this (meaning, by performing *yajñas*); and may those gods be kind to you; thus, fostering one another, you will attain the supreme good.

Life (*āyuḥ*) is continued through life – parents to children. *Āyuḥ* may also be translated as longevity.

Truth is protected by persons living a truthful life.

Similarly, Dharma is protected by persons living their lives based on Dharma. [1]*Dharmo rakṣati rakṣitaḥ* (धर्मो रक्षति रक्षित:) – one who protects Dharma is protected by Dharma. What is Dharma? Erroneously, Dharma is translated as religion.

According to the *Manu-Smṛti* VI.92:

धृति: क्षमा दमोऽस्तेयं शौचमिन्द्रिय-निग्रह: |
धीर्विद्या सत्यमक्रोधो दशकं धर्मलक्षणम् ||

Dhṛtiḥ kṣamā damo'steyaṁ śauca-mindriya-nigrahaḥ |
Dhīr-vidyā satyamakrodho daśakaṁ dharma-lakṣaṇam ||

> The ten signs of Dharma are – fortitude, forgiveness, control of mind, not stealing (honesty), cleanliness of body and purity of mind, control of sense organs (self-control), wisdom, acquisition of knowledge, truthfulness, and absence of anger.

Our scriptures also talk about compassion, charity, non-violence, humility, absence of hatred, austerity, sacrifice, etc., as part of Dharma. Dharma also includes fulfilling duties towards family, society, nation, all living beings, and nature – environment, protection of trees, etc.

---

[1]*Mahābhārata*, *Vanaparva*, Chapter 313, Verse 128

Faith in God, the study of scriptures, physical exercises (e.g., *Haṭha* Yoga), religious practices (worship and prayers), spiritual practices (*sādhanā*), etc., are one's Dharma for own progress – worldly as well as spiritual. Such a person will have no problem in following his Dharma towards others as described above; he will always remain peaceful and serene. He will eventually be free from the shackles of worldly bondage and the cycles of births and deaths (i.e., he will be liberated or will attain *mokṣa* or *nirvāṇa*).

Chapter 16 of *Śrīmad Bhagavad Gītā* discusses divine qualities – Fearlessness, purity of heart, steadfastness in knowledge and yoga, charity, control over the mind, *yajña* (worship and performance of sacrifice), the study of scriptures, austerity, simplicity, non-violence, truthfulness, absence of anger, sacrifice, serenity, lack of cruelty, compassion, un-covetousness, gentleness, modesty, firmness, vigor, forgiveness, fortitude, cleanliness, absence of hatred, and absence of desire to be honored by others. These qualities are part of Dharma, which shows that a person who follows his Dharma is, in fact, a divine person.

1.4 [1]**ततो ह वै ते देवा रुद्रमपृच्छन् ते देवा रुद्रमपश्यन् ते देवा रुद्रमध्यायन् ते देवा ऊर्ध्वबाहवो रुद्रं स्तुवन्ति ॥ १ ॥**

---

[1]ते देवाः परमात्मानं रुद्रं ध्यायन्ति शंकरम् ॥ Liṅga II.17.23
Te devāḥ paramātmanaṁ Rudraṁ dhyāyanti Śaṅkaram ||

सनारायणका देवाः सेंद्राश्च मुनयस्तथा ।
तथोर्ध्वबाहवो देवा रुद्रं स्तुन्वन्ति शंकरम् ॥ Liṅga II.17.24
Sa-Nārāyaṇakā devāḥ sendrāśca munayas-tathā |

Tato ha vai te devā Rudra-mapṛcchan te devā Raudra-mapaśyan te devā Rudra-madhyāyan te devā ūrdhava-bāhavo Rudraṁ stuvanti ||1||

> [Hearing this,] the gods asked Rudra, looked at Him, meditated upon Him, and then raised their arms and praised Him [with the hymn of praise given in the next mantra]. ||1||

The literal meaning of the word '*apṛcchan*' is 'asked a question.' But, as you see in the Mantra, gods really asked no question. Instead, there were questions in their eyes to know how great Rudra was; they were astonished to see Him. They looked at Him with amused and puzzled eyes and started praising Him.

|| Thus, ends Mantra 1 ||

|| ॐ ||

Tathordhva-bāhavo devā Rudraṁ stunvanti Śaṅkaram ||

Mantra 2

Mantra 2 is the glorification of Lord Rudra by gods. As stated in Mantra 1.4, though gods are looking at Rudra and reciting this hymn in His praise, He is addressed in the third person, instead of second, which is very common in Sanskrit literature.

According to this hymn, the whole universe, including all the gods (*devas*) – everything is Rudra's manifestation.

2.1 [1]ॐ यो वै रुद्रः स भगवान् यश्च ब्रह्मा तस्मै वै नमो नमः ।१॥

Om Yo vai Rudraḥ sa bhagavān yaśca Brahmā tasmai vai namo namaḥ |1||

---

[1]देवा ऊचुः ॥ *Devā ūcuḥ* ||

य एष भगवान् रुद्रो ब्रह्मविष्णुमहेश्वराः ।
स्कन्दश्चापि तथा चेन्द्रो भुवनानि चतुर्दश ।
अश्विनौ ग्रहताराश्च नक्षत्राणि च खं दिशः ॥ Liṅga II.18.1
Ya eṣa bhagavān Rudro Brahma-Viṣṇu-Maheśvarāḥ |
Skandaś-cāpi tathā cendro bhuvanāni catur-daśa |
Aśvinau graha-tārāśca nakṣatrāṇi ca khaṁ diśaḥ ||

भूतानि च तथा सूर्यः सोमश्चाष्टौ ग्रहास्तथा । Liṅga II.18.2
Bhūtāni ca tathā sūryaḥ somaś-cāṣṭau grahās-tathā |

> Om. He who is Rudra is verily God; He is *Brahmā* (the creator), [and] prostrations to Him again and again.

The word *bhagavān* (or *bhagavat*) has many meanings. As an adjective, it means prosperous, happy, glorious, venerable, divine, exalted one, etc. It also means one who possesses fortunes. To show reverence, saints, sages, and gods are also addressed as *Bhagavān*. As a noun, it is used as God. In this hymn, since Rudra is worshipped as the god of gods, I have translated *Bhagavān* as God.

2.2 यो वै रुद्रः स भगवान् यश्च विष्णुस्तस्मै वै नमो नमः ।२॥

Yo vai Rudraḥ sa bhagavān yaśca Viṣṇus-tasmai vai namo namaḥ |2||

> He who is Rudra is verily God; He is *Viṣṇu* (the preserver), [and] prostrations to Him again and again.

2.3 यो वै रुद्रः स भगवान् यश्च स्कन्दस्तस्मै वै नमो नमः ।३॥

Yo vai Rudraḥ sa bhagavān yaśca Skandas-tasmai vai namo namaḥ |3||

> He who is Rudra is verily God; He is *Skanda* (the commander of the army of gods – *devas* – and son of Lord Śiva), [and] prostrations to Him again and again.

2.4 यो वै रुद्रः स भगवान् यश्चेन्द्रस्तस्मै वै नमो नमः ।४॥

Yo vai Rudraḥ sa bhagavān yaścendras-tasmai vai namo namaḥ |4||

He who is Rudra is verily God; He is *Indra* (Chief of gods), [and] prostrations to Him again and again.

2.5 यो वै रुद्रः स भगवान् यश्चाग्निस्तस्मै वै नमो नमः |५||

Yo vai Rudraḥ sa bhagavān yaścāgnis-tasmai vai namo namaḥ |5||

He who is Rudra is verily God; He is *Agni* (Fire-god), [and] prostrations to Him again and again.

2.6 यो वै रुद्रः स भगवान् यश्च वायुस्तस्मै वै नमो नमः |६||

Yo vai Rudraḥ sa bhagavān yaśca Vāyus-tasmai vai namo namaḥ |6||

He who is Rudra is verily God; He is *Vāyu* (Air-god – Wind), [and] prostrations to Him again and again.

2.7 यो वै रुद्रः स भगवान् यश्च सूर्यस्तस्मै वै नमो नमः |७||

Yo vai Rudraḥ sa bhagavān yaśca sūryas-tasmai vai namo namaḥ |7||

He who is Rudra is verily God; He is *Sūrya* (Sun-god), [and] prostrations to Him again and again.

2.8 यो वै रुद्रः स भगवान् यश्च सोमस्तस्मै वै नमो नमः ।८॥

Yo vai Rudraḥ sa bhagavān yaśca somas-tasmai vai namo namaḥ |8||

He who is Rudra is verily God; He is *Soma* (or *Candra*, Moon-god), [and] prostrations to Him again and again.

2.9 यो वै रुद्रः स भगवान् ये चाष्टौ ग्रहास्तस्मै वै नमो नमः ।९॥

Yo vai Rudraḥ sa bhagavān ye cāṣṭau grahās-tasmai vai namo namaḥ |9||

He who is Rudra is verily God; He is the eight *grahas*, [and] prostrations to Him again and again.

2.10 यो वै रुद्रः स भगवान् ये चाष्टौ प्रतिग्रहास्तस्मै वै नमो नमः ।१०॥

Yo vai Rudraḥ sa bhagavān ye cāṣṭau prati-grahās-tasmai vai namo namaḥ |10||

> He who is Rudra is verily God; He is the *eight prati-grahas*, [and] prostrations to Him again and again.

According to the Śiva *Purāṇa*, *Śata-Rudra-Saṁhitā* (शिवपुराण, शतरुद्रसंहिता), Chapter II, Verses 2 to 4, Lord Śiva, by pervading the universe, holds its objects together in balance the way pearls are held together by a string. Lord Śiva has eight forms: *Śarva* (शर्व), *Bhava* (भव), *Rudra* (रुद्र), *Ugra* (उग्र), *Bhīma* (भीम), *Paśupati* (पशुपति), *Īśāna* (ईशान), and *Mahādeva* (महादेव). They respectively are the presiding deities of Earth (*Prithivī* पृथिवी), Water (*Jala* जल), Fire (*Agni* अग्नि), Air (*Vāyu* वायु), Space (*Akāśa* आकाश), Individual self (*Jīvātman* जीवात्मन्), Sun (*Sūrya* सूर्य), and Moon (*Candra* चन्द्र). Earth, Water, Fire, Air, and Space are the five elements, known as *Pañca-tattva* (पञ्चतत्त्व) or *Pañca-bhūta* (पञ्चभूत).

Grahas (ग्रहा:): *Graha* means, 'one which is seized or taken hold off' – *Gṛhyate iti grahaḥ* (गृह्यते इति ग्रह:). Earth, Water, Fire, Air, Space, *Jivātman* (individual self), Sun, and Moon are the *Grahas*; they are reigned by Lord Śiva through His eight forms. Lord Śiva manifests Himself through these eight *Grahas*.

Pratigrahas (प्रतिग्रहा:): 'One who is comprehended is *Pratigraha' – Pratigṛhyate iti Pratigrahaḥ* (प्रतिगृह्यते इति ग्रह:). Lord Śiva is comprehended or understood by His devotees through these eight forms, and therefore, they are called *Prarigrahas*. See Table II.1.

TABLE II.1

No.	***Graha*** **(ग्रह)**	***Pratigraha*** **(प्रतिग्रह)** **(Presiding Deity)**
1	Earth (*Prithivī* पृथिवी)	*Śarva* (शर्व)
2	Water (*Jala* जल)	*Bhava* (भव)
3	Fire (*Agni* अग्नि)	*Rudra* (रुद्र)
4	Air (*Vāyu* वायु)	*Ugra* (उग्र)
5	Space (*Akāśa* आकाश)	*Bhīma* (भीम)
6	Individual self (*Jīvātman* जीवात्मन्)	*Paśupati* (पशुपति)
7	Sun (*Sūrya* सूर्य)	*Īśāna* (ईशान)
8	Moon (*Candra* चन्द्र)	*Mahādeva* (महादेव)

Now, I will explain the eight *Grahas* in a different way. There are eleven senses (*Indriyāṇi* - इन्द्रयाणि) – one mind, five organs of perception or knowledge (*Jñānendriyāṇi* - ज्ञानेन्द्रियाणि), and five organs of action (*Karmendriyāṇi* - कर्मेन्द्रियाणि). They are shown below:

(i) Mind (Manas – मनस्).

(ii) Five organs of perception or knowledge (*Jñānendriyāṇi* - ज्ञानेन्द्रियाणि)

   a. Nose (*Ghrāṇa* - घ्राण)
   b. Tongue (*Jihvā* - जिह्वा)
   c. Eyes (*Cakṣu* - चक्षु)
   d. Skin (*Tvac* - त्वच्)
   e. Ears (*Śrotra* - श्रोत्र)

(iii) Five organs of action (*Karmendriyāṇi* - कर्मेन्द्रियाणि)

   a. Larynx (*Vāc* - वाच्)
   b. Hands (*Kara* - कर)
   c. Feet (*Pāda* - पाद)
   d. The organ of generation (*Upastha* - उपस्थ)
   e. The organ of excretion (*Pāyu* - पायु)

The mind's function is to desire (*Kāma* - काम).

Each organ of knowledge has an object of perception, as shown below:

   a. Nose → Smell (*Gandha* - गन्ध)
   b. Tongue → Taste (*Rasa* - रस)
   c. Eyes → Sight or Form/Shape (*Rūpa* - रूप)
   d. Skin → Touch (*Sparśa* - स्पर्श)

e. Ears → Sound (*Śabda* - शब्द)

Each organ of action has an activity or work to be done, as shown below:

a. Larynx → Speech (*Nāma* - नाम)
b. Hands → Work (*Karma* - कर्म)
c. Feet → Move
d. The organ of generation → to generate
e. The organ of excretion → to excrete

Eight *Grahas* (ग्रहाः) and Eight *Atigrahas* (अतिग्रहाः): Here, *Graha* means one that seizes or grasps, meaning seizer. *Atigraha* means super seizer. According to the *Bṛhadāraṇyaka Upaniṣad* (बृहदारण्यक उपनिषद्) III.2.2-9, there are eight *Grahas* and corresponding eight *Atigrahas*. The eight *Grahas* are: (i) Five organs of knowledge, (ii) Mind, and (iii) The first two organs of action. Thus, the eight *Grahas* are – (i) Nose, (ii) Tongue, (iii) Eyes, (iv) Skin, (v) Ears, (vi) Mind, (vii) Larynx, and (viii) Hands. These eight *Grahas* are respectively dominated or seized (*Gṛhīta* गृहीत) by the eight *Atigrahas*, which are their corresponding functions: (i) Smell, (ii) Taste, (iii) Sight or Form/Shape, (iv) Touch, (v) Sound, (vi) Desire, (vii) Speech, and (viii) Work.

A person connects to the outer world through the eight *Grahas* (nose, tongue, eyes, etc.). Through them, he seizes or grasps or experiences the outer world. His experiences consist of the smell, taste, form/shape, etc. (which are *Atigrahas*) of the outer world objects. He enjoys the objects when he likes their smell, taste, shape, etc. and hates them when he does not like them. Thus, he becomes a slave of the *Atigrahas*, which are the functions of his *Grahas*. As a result, instead of enjoying the world through these senses, he suffers because they (meaning A*tigrahas*) rule over him; instead of grabbing them, they grab him. Therefore, the *Atigrahas* may also be named as *Pratigrahas*, because they grab back. The Sanskrit word *Prati* means back, in return, against, etc.

Table II.2 summarizes the eight *Grahas* and corresponding *Atigrahas/Pratigrahas*.

TABLE II.2

Graha **(ग्रह)**	***Atigraha/Pratigraha*** **(अतिग्रह/प्रतिग्रह)**
Nose (*Ghrāṇa* - घ्राण)	Smell (*Gandha* - गन्ध)
Tongue (*Jihvā* - जिह्वा)	Taste (*Rasa* - रस)
Eyes (*Cakṣu* - चक्षु)	Sight or Form/Shape (*Rūpa* - रूप)
Skin (*Tvac* - त्वच्)	Touch (*Sparśa* - स्पर्श)
Ears (*Śrotra* - श्रोत्र)	Sound (*Śabda* - शब्द)
Mind (*Manas* - मनस्)	Desires (*Kāma* - काम)
Larynx (*Vāc* - वाच्)	Speech (*Nāma* - नाम)
Hands (*Kara* - कर)	Work (*Karma* - कर्म)

2.11 [1]**यो वै रुद्रः स भगवान् यच्च भूस्तस्मै वै नमो नमः ।११॥**

---

[1]त्वमादौ च तथा भूतो भूर्भुवःस्वस्तथैव च । Linga II.18.4
Tvamādau ca tathā bhūto bhūr-buvaḥ-svas-tathaiva ca |

Yo vai Rudraḥ sa bhagavān yacca bhūs-tasmai vai namo namaḥ |11||

> He who is Rudra is verily God; He is this world, [and] prostrations to Him again and again.

2.12 यो वै रुद्रः स भगवान् यच्च भुवस्तस्मै वै नमो नमः |१२||

Yo vai Rudraḥ sa bhagavān yacca bhuvas-tasmai vai namo namaḥ |12||

> He who is Rudra is verily God; He is *Bhuvaḥ* (mid-region, the world between this world and Heaven), [and] prostrations to Him again and again.

2.13 यो वै रुद्रः स भगवान् यच्च स्वस्तस्मै वै नमो नमः |१३||

Yo vai Rudraḥ sa bhagavān yacca svas-tasmai vai namo namaḥ |13||

> He who is Rudra is verily God; He is the Heaven, [and] prostrations to Him again and again.

2.14 यो वै रुद्रः स भगवान् यच्च महस्तस्मै वै नमो नमः |१४||

Yo vai Rudraḥ sa bhagavān yacca mahas-tasmai vai namo namaḥ |14||

> He who is Rudra is verily God; He is *Mahaḥ,* [and] prostrations to Him again and again.

There are 14 worlds or planes of existence (*Lokas*) – seven higher worlds and seven lower worlds. Only the first four higher worlds are mentioned in this hymn (Mantras 2.11 to 2.14). All the 14 worlds are Rudra's manifestation.

Higher Worlds

From the lowest to the highest, the seven higher worlds (*Lokas*) are – *Bhuḥ* (भूः), *Bhuvaḥ* (भुवः), *Svaḥ* (स्वः), *Mahaḥ* (महः), *Janaḥ* (जनः), *Tapaḥ* (तपः), and *Satyam* (सत्यम्). *Bhuḥ* is the world where we live, and *Svaḥ* is *Svarloka*, meaning heaven; *Bhuvaḥ* is the world in-between. When *Jīvaātman* (जीवात्मन्), the individual self, keeps evolving or spiritually progressing, he goes from the lower to the higher planes of existence.

Sapta-Vyāhṛtis (सप्तव्याहृतयः)

Bhuḥ, *Bhuvaḥ*, *Svaḥ*, *Mahaḥ*, *Janaḥ*, *Tapaḥ,* and *Satyam* – these are also called *sapta-vyāhṛtis* (meaning, seven mystical utterances). They are called utterances because they are mentally uttered (*Japa* जप) during *prāṇāyāma* (Yoga of breathing, loosely translated as a breathing exercise).

Prāṇāyāma (प्राणायाम) Mantra:

ॐ भूः । ॐ भुवः । ॐ स्वः । ॐ महः । ॐ जनः । ॐ तपः । ॐ सत्यम् । ॐ तत्सवितुर्वरेण्यं भर्गो देवस्य धीमहि । धियो यो नः प्रचोदयात् । ॐ आपो ज्योती रसोऽमृतं ब्रह्म भूर्भुवः स्वरोम् ॥

Om Bhuḥ | Om Bhuvaḥ | Om Svaḥ | Om Mahaḥ | Om Janaḥ | Om Tapaḥ | Om Satyam | Om Tat savitur-vareṇyaṁ bhargo devasya dhīmahi | Dhiyo yo naḥ pracodayāt || Om āpo jyotī raso'mṛtaṁ brahma bhūrbhuvaḥ svarom |

The procedure for doing *prāṇāyāma*:

Pūraka (पूरक) – inhalation: The recitation of the mantra is to be done mentally. Use your right hand. With your thumb, close the right nostril and breathe in with your left nostril while reciting the *prāṇāyāma* mantra. This is called *Pūraka* – inhalation.

Kumbhaka *(कुम्भक)* – retention: Now, close both nostrils, the right one with the thumb and the left one with the little and ring fingers, and hold your breath while reciting the mantra;

your index and middle fingers should point upwards. This is called *Kumbhaka* – retention.

***Recaka* (रेचक) – exhalation:** Now, release the thumb (the left nostril must still be closed), and breathe out with your right nostril while reciting the mantra. This is called *Recaka* – exhalation.

With your left nostril still closed, breathe in with your right nostril while reciting the mantra (*Pūraka*; inhalation); then close both nostrils and hold the breath while reciting the mantra (*Kumbhaka*; retention); release the left nostril while the right nostril is still closed, and breathe out with the left nostril, while chanting the mantra (*Recaka*; exhalation).

This is one *prāṇāyāma*.

While you are doing *prāṇāyāma*, keep your eyes closed and focus your eyes on the spot between your two eyebrows, which is called *Ājñā Cakra* (आज्ञा चक्र). If you believe in a personal God or Goddess (*Iṣṭa-devatā* इष्टदेवता, meaning personal Deity like Śiva, *Kṛṣṇa*, *Durgā*, etc.), instead of focusing on the *Ājñā Cakra*, you may concentrate on your *Iṣṭa-deva* situated in your heart (*hṛdaya* हृदय); it is called *Anāhata Cakra* (अनाहत चक्र). When I say heart, it is not your physical heart; instead, it the spot located at the level of the heart, at the center of the chest; this is known as the cavity of the heart.

Start with one *prāṇāyāma* at a time, and then gradually increase the number. If you increase suddenly, you may feel dizzy and harm your health.

Alternatively, if it is hard to recite the entire mantra, especially for beginners, the aspirant may chant only the following part:

> ॐ भूः । ॐ भुवः । ॐ स्वः । ॐ महः । ॐ जनः । ॐ तपः । ॐ सत्यम् । ॐ तत्सवितुर्वरेण्यं भर्गो देवस्य धीमहि । धियो यो नः प्रचोदयात् ।
>
> *Om Bhuḥ | Om Bhuvaḥ | Om Svaḥ | Om Mahaḥ | Om Janaḥ | Om Tapaḥ | Om Satyam | Om Tat savitur-vareṇyaṁ bhargo devasya dhīmahi | Dhiyo yo naḥ pracodayāt ||*

If even this is difficult, the aspirant may recite only the *Gāyatrī* (गायत्री) mantra:

> ॐ भूर्भुवः स्वः । तत्सवितुर्वरेण्यं भर्गो देवस्य धीमहि । धियो यो नः प्रचोदयात् ।
>
> *Om Bhūr-bhuvaḥ-svaḥ | Tat savitur-vareṇyaṁ bhargo devasya dhīmahi | Dhiyo yo naḥ pracodayāt ||*

Mahā-Vyāhṛtis (महाव्याहृतयः)

The first three worlds of the *Sapta-vyāhṛtis* – *Bhuḥ*, *Bhuvaḥ*, *Svaḥ* – are known as *mahā-vyāhṛtis* (great *vyāhṛtis*), because these are the main ones. The *mahā-vyāhṛtis* are uttered before reciting many mantras, especially the *Gāyatrī* mantra.

Gāyatrī Mantra (गायत्री मन्त्र)

The *Gāyatrī* mantra is the most powerful and sacred Vedic mantra. It is a prayer to *Brahman*, the Supreme Reality, for enlightenment. The *Gāyatrī* mantra is written in the *Gāyatrī* meter, which has three *pādas* (feet पाद), each *pāda* having eight syllables (*akṣara* अक्षर); thus, the *Gāyatrī* mantra has a total of 24 syllables. The mantra is originally given in the *Ṛgveda* III.62.10; the mantra was revealed to Great Sage *Viśvāmitra* (विश्वामित्र) during his deep meditation. Here is the mantra:

तत्सवितुर्वरेण्यं भर्गो देवस्य धीमहि । धियो यो नः प्रचोदयात् ।

Tat savitur-vareṇyaṁ bhargo devasya dhīmahi | Dhiyo yo naḥ pracodayāt ||

Its three *pādas*, each having eight syllables, are given below:

1 2 3 4 5 6 7 8
Tat sa-vi-tur va-re-ṇ-yaṁ

1 2 3 4 5 6 7 8
Bhar-go de-vas-ya dhī-ma-hi |

1 2 3 4 5 6 7 8
Dhi-yo yo naḥ pra-co-da-yāt ||

The *Gāyatrī* mantra is the mother of the Vedas, and the *Gāyatrī* meter is the mother of all meters. It is called *Gāyatrī* because it is sung (गीयते *gīyate*).

The *Chāndogya Upaniṣad* III.12.1 glorifies *Gāyatrī* saying: All this whatever exists is indeed *Gāyatrī*. Speech indeed is *Gāyatrī* because it sings and protects [from the fear of whatever exists].

> Note: Here, *Gāyatrī* stands for *gāyati* (sings, गायति) and *trāyate* (protects, त्रायते).

In the *Bhagavad-Gītā* X.35, *Śrī Kṛṣṇa* says, "*Gāyatrī chandasāmaham* (गायत्री छन्दसामहम्) – among the Vedic hymns, I am the *Gāyatrī hymn.*" Thus, *Gāyatrī* hymn is identified with Lord *Kṛṣṇa*, who is the personification of *Brahman*, the Highest Truth.

Gāyatrī Mantra *Japa* (जप)

Japa is the repetition of a mantra again and again. The *Gāyatrī japa* destroys all sins; it gives the same fruits that are acquired by reciting the Vedas. It blesses the aspirant with good health, vigor, prosperity, and spiritual enlightenment. During *japa*, before the actual *Gāyatrī* mantra is chanted, Om and *Mahāvyāhṛtis* are recited first, as shown below:

> ॐ भूर्भुवः स्वः । तत्सवितुर्वरेण्यं भर्गो देवस्य धीमहि ।
> धियो यो नः प्रचोदयात् ।
>
> *Om Bhūr-bhuvaḥ-svaḥ | Tat savitur-vareṇyaṁ bhargo devasya dhīmahi | Dhiyo yo naḥ pracodayāt ||*

Śukla Yajurveda 36.3

(**Om**) *Brahman* (Absolute God) is (***Bhūr***) the source of all existence and the support of all, (***Bhuvaḥ***) the remover of afflictions, and (***Svaḥ***) all-pervading, who bestows bliss upon all. (***Dhīmahi***) Let us meditate upon the (***Vareṇyam***) adorable (***Bhargo***) radiance of (***Tat***) that (***Savitur***) Self-Illuminating and brilliant (***Devasya***) Supreme Divine Being, (***Yo***) who may (***Pracodayāt***) enlighten (***Naḥ***) our (***Dhiyo***) intellect [so that we may live righteously and realize the Supreme Truth].

Explanation of the meaning

According to the *Taittirīya Upaniṣad* (तैत्तिरीय उपनिषद्), I.5, *Bhūriti vai prāṇaḥ, Bhuva ityapānaḥ, suvariti vyānaḥ* (भूरिति वै प्राणः। भुव इत्यपानः। सुवरिति व्यानः।) – *Bhū* is indeed *Prāṇa*; *Bhuva* is *Apāna*; *Suva* is *Vyāna.*

There are five *Prāṇas* – *Prāṇa*, *Apāna*, *Vyāna*, *Udāna*, and *Samāna*. These are the vital airs or energies in our body that keep our body and mind healthy and functioning. For more details, see the commentary on Mantra 4.1.

There are two *Yajurvedas* – *Śukla Yajurveda* (शुक्लयजुर्वेद) and *Kṛṣṇa Yajurveda* (कृष्णयजुर्वेद). The *Taittirīya Upaniṣad* belongs to the *Kṛṣṇa Yajurveda*. The third *vyāhṛti*, which is *Svaḥ* (स्वः) in the *Śukla Yajurveda*, is written as *Suvaḥ* (सुवः) in the *Kṛṣṇa Yajurveda*. Thus, *Svaḥ* or *Suvaḥ* is *Vyāna.*

Om – Om, or the symbol ॐ, is synonymous with *Brahman*, the Ultimate Truth.

Bhūr or *Bhūḥ* – It is another name of earth.

1. The earth is the reason we exist; therefore, it is the source of existence.
2. *Bhū* is indeed *Prāṇa* – *Bhū* or the earth is *Prāṇa*; *Prāṇa* being life energy supports all.

Therefore, I have translated *Bhūr* as the source of all existence and the support of all.

Bhuvaḥ – It is the mid-region, the world between the earth and heaven.

1. *Bhuva* includes the earth's atmosphere, which gives us air and rain. The rain produces food and herbs, which nourish us and keep us healthy. They remove our illnesses or afflictions.
2. *Bhuva* is *Apāna* – *Apāna* being one of the vital energies, keeps us healthy.

Therefore, I have translated *Bhuvaḥ* as the remover of afflictions.

Svaḥ – It is another name of heaven.

1. Heaven gives us pleasure or bliss.
2. *Sva* is *Vyāna* – *Vyāna* is the vital energy that is spread all around the body and keeps all the arteries and nerves functioning and thus keeps the body healthy. *Vyān* also stands for *Vyāpaka* (व्यापक), meaning all-pervading.

Therefore, I have translated *Svaḥ* as all-pervading, who bestows bliss upon all.

Tat – *Tat* means that; it refers to *Savitā* (see below).

Savitur or *Savituḥ* – It is the genitive case of '*Savitṛ*.' *Savitṛ* or *Savitā* is another name of the sun, which stands for self-effulgent and brilliant.

Vareṇyam – adorable; worthy to be worshiped.

Bhargo or *Bhargaḥ* – radiance.

Devasya – It is the genitive case of *Deva*. *Devasya* means 'of the Divine Being.'

Dhīmahi – It means 'Let us meditate upon.'

Dhiyo or *Dhiyaḥ* – It is plural of *Dhī*, meaning the intelligence or wisdom. I have translated it in singular instead of the plural to keep the sentence simple.

Yo or *Yaḥ* – who.

Naḥ – ours.

Pracodayāt – It means, 'May He (meaning *Brahman*) inspire.' I have translated it as enlighten.

Lower Worlds

From the highest to the lowest, the seven lower worlds are – *Atala* (अतल), *Vitala* (वितल), *Sutala* (सुतल), *Talātala* (तलातल), *Rasātala* (रसातल), *Mahātala* (महातल), and *Pātāla*

(पाताल). *Tala* means bottom. When the soul keeps spiritually falling, it goes to the lower worlds.

Outer World and Inner World

The universe is called *Brahmāṇḍa* (ब्रह्मार्माण्ड) and this body is called *Piṇḍa* (पिण्ड). The Vedic (Hindu) scriptures say that what you find outside in the *Brahmāṇḍa*, you will also find inside the *Piṇḍa*. In fact, I would say that what you see outside is a lot smaller than the world that exists inside. You see the sky (*Ākāśa* - आकाश) outside of you; similarly, there is a sky inside too, which is called *Cidākāśa* (चिदाकाश). *Cit* (चित्) means Consciousness, and *ākāśa* means sky or space. Since the [1]Consciousness is all-pervading, all-knowing, and ever-existing, it is infinite and timeless. Whereas the outside world consisting of planets, stars, galaxies, time, space, etc., is limited and time-bound, hence, it is smaller.

The same 14 worlds are situated inside the human body too. There are 14 *cakras* in the body, seven upper ones, and seven lower ones. Literally, *Cakra* (चक्र) means wheel, it is the wheel of energy. The energy in the upper *cakras* is positive, whereas the energy in the lower *cakras* is negative. The book 'Dancing with Śiva, Pg. 699 (see Bibliography)' defines *cakra*

---

[1] Ordinarily, consciousness means awareness, whereas, in spirituality, it means *Cit*, the all-knowing aspect of *Brahman* – *Sat-Cit-Ānanda* (Existence-Consciousness-Bliss).

as "any of the nerve plexes [plexuses?] or centers of force and consciousness located within the inner bodies of man."

The seven upper *cakras*, from the lowest to the highest, are – *Mūlādhāra* (मूलाधार, located at the base of the spine), *Svādhiṣṭhāna* (स्वाधिष्ठान, below the navel), *Maṇipura* (मणिपुर, navel), *Anāhata* (अनाहत, located at the center of the chest at the level of the heart), *Viśuddha* (विशुद्ध, throat), *Ājñā* (आज्ञा, between the eyebrows), and *Sahasrāra* (सहस्रार, the crown of the head). The worlds *Bhuḥ*, *Bhuvaḥ*, *Svaḥ*, *Mahaḥ*, *Janaḥ*, *Tapaḥ,* and *Satyam* are respectively located in *Mūlādhāra*, *Svādhiṣṭhāna*, *Maṇipura*, *Anāhata*, *Viśuddha*, *Ājñā,* and *Sahasrāra cakras*.

Tapaḥ is also known as *Siddha-Loka* (सिद्धलोक), where *Siddhas* reside. *Siddhas* are the great souls who have achieved spiritual perfection through enormous *tapa* (austerity). This is the reason during meditation yogĩs focus their eyes on the space between the two eyebrows, i.e., the *Ājñā Cakra*.

The *Satyam* or the *Satya-Loka* (सत्यलोक) is also known as *Brahma-Loka* (ब्रह्मलोक) since this is the highest *Loka* or world. *Śakti* (शक्ति), the divine energy, lives in the *Mūlādhāra Cakra*. With constant spiritual practice, the yogĩ brings *Śakti*, step-by-step, to the *Sahasrāra Cakra*, where she joins Śiva, Her consort, the highest state of existence.

The seven lower *cakras Atala* (अतल), *Vitala* (वितल), *Sutala* (सुतल), *Talātala* (तलातल), *Rasātala* (रसातल), *Mahātala*

(महातल), and *Pātāla* (पाताल) are respectively located at the hips, thighs, knees, calves, ankles, feet, and the soles of the feet.

2.15 यो वै रुद्रः स भगवान् या च पृथिवी तस्मै वै नमो नमः |१५||

Yo vai Rudraḥ sa bhagavān yā ca pṛthivī tasmai vai namo namaḥ |15||

> He who is Rudra is verily God; He is the earth,
> [and] prostrations to Him again and again.

The world is made up of five elements – earth, water, fire, air, and space. These elements are called *tattvas* in Sanskrit. Together, they are called *pañca-būtas* or *pañca-tattvas*, meaning five-elements; *pañca* (पञ्च) means five and *bhūta* (भूत) means element. It should be noted that space, though it is subtle and cannot be heard, touched, seen, or tasted, is still called an element since it is part of nature, not a part of the Consciousness. Similarly, the light and the heat, though according to the science, are considered energies, are part of the fire element.

2.16 यो वै रुद्रः स भगवान् यच्चान्तरिक्षं तस्मै वै नमो नमः |१६||

Yo vai Rudraḥ sa bhagavān yaccāntarikṣaṁ tasmai vai namo namaḥ |16||

> He who is Rudra is verily God; He is the mid-region (atmosphere), [and] prostrations to Him again and again.

2.17 यो वै रुद्रः स भगवान् या च द्यौस्तस्मै वै नमो नमः ।१७॥

Yo vai Rudraḥ sa bhagavān yā ca dyaus-tasmai vai namo namaḥ |17||

> He who is Rudra is verily God; He is the Heaven, [and] prostrations to Him again and again.

2.18 यो वै रुद्रः स भगवान् याश्चापस्तस्मै वै नमो नमः ।१८॥

Yo vai Rudraḥ sa bhagavān yāścāpas-tasmai vai namo namaḥ |18||

> He who is Rudra is verily God; He is the water, [and] prostrations to Him again and again.

Ap (अप्) means water, *āpas* (आपस्) or *āpaḥ* (आपः) is its plural; commonly, it is used in plural form. *Ap* is feminine gender.

2.19 यो वै रुद्रः स भगवान् यच्च तेजस्तस्मै वै नमो नमः ।१९॥

Yo vai Rudraḥ sa bhagavān yacca tejas-tasmai vai namo namaḥ |19||

He who is Rudra is verily God; He is the light (or radiance or fire), [and] prostrations to Him again and again.

2.20 [1]**यो वै रुद्रः स भगवान् यश्च कालस्तस्मै वै नमो नमः |२०||**

Yo vai Rudraḥ sa bhagavān yaśca kālas-tasmai vai namo namaḥ |20||

He who is Rudra is verily God; He is the Time, [and] prostrations to Him again and again.

2.21 यो वै रुद्रः स भगवान् यश्च यमस्तस्मै वै नमो नमः |२१||

Yo vai Rudraḥ sa bhagavān yaśca yamas-tasmai vai namo namaḥ |21||

He who is Rudra is verily God; He is the god of death, [and] prostrations to Him again and again.

2.22 यो वै रुद्रः स भगवान् यश्च मृत्युस्तस्मै वै नमो नमः |२२||

Yo vai Rudraḥ sa bhagavān yaśca mṛtyus-tasmai vai namo namaḥ |22||

---

[1] [1]प्राणः कालो यमो मृत्युरमृतः परमेश्वरः || Liṅga II.18.2
Prāṇaḥ kālo yamo mṛtyuramṛtaḥ Parameśvaraḥ ||

He who is Rudra is verily God; He is the death, [and] we bow down to Him again and again.

2.23 यो वै रुद्रः स भगवान् यच्चामृतं तस्मै वै नमो नमः ।२३॥

Yo vai Rudraḥ sa bhagavān yaccāmṛtaṁ tasmai vai namo namaḥ |23||

He who is Rudra is verily God; He is the nectar (ambrosia), [and] prostrations to Him again and again.

As mentioned in Mantras 2.20 to 2.22, Lord Rudra's names are *Kāla* (Time), *Yama* (God of death), and *Mṛtyu* (Death). These three names are related to death.

Literally, *kāla* means time. [1]Lord Śiva as *Brahmā* creates the world, as *Viṣṇu* maintains it, and as Rudra destroys it. When He destroys the world, He is called *Kāla*, the annihilator, the god of death. Lord Śiva is called Time because the time began when He created this world and the time will end when He will annihilate it. Thus, *Kāla* (Time), Death, or the god of death are appropriate names for Śiva.

Lord Rudra is also called *Amṛta*, meaning nectar, which gives immortality. Of course, anyone who takes birth will undoubtedly die. Immortality means attaining *mokṣa* or liberation, after which there is no more birth and death.

---

[1] According to the *Śiva-Mahā-Purāṇa*, *Vidyeśvara-Saṁhitā* Chapter 10

2.24 यो वै रुद्रः स भगवान् यच्चाकाशं तस्मै वै नमो नमः |२४||

Yo vai Rudraḥ sa bhagavān yaccā-kāśaṁ tasmai vai namo namaḥ |24||

He who is Rudra is verily God; He is the sky (or space), [and] prostrations to Him again and again.

2.25 यो वै रुद्रः स भगवान् यच्च विश्वं तस्मै वै नमो नमः |२५||

Yo vai Rudraḥ sa bhagavān yacca viśvaṁ tasmai vai namo namaḥ |25||

He who is Rudra is verily God; He is the world, [and] prostrations to Him again and again.

Viśva also means whole, entire, all-pervading. Rudra is everything and everywhere.

2.26 यो वै रुद्रः स भगवान् यच्च स्थूलं तस्मै वै नमो नमः |२६||

Yo vai Rudraḥ sa bhagavān yacca sthūlaṁ tasmai vai namo namaḥ |26||

He who is Rudra is verily God; He is gross (meaning all that is visible, or one having a physical form; it is the opposite of subtle), [and] prostrations to Him again and again.

2.27 यो वै रुद्रः स भगवान् यच्च सूक्ष्मं तस्मै वै नमो नमः ।२७॥

Yo vai Rudraḥ sa bhagavān yacca sūkṣmaṁ tasmai vai namo namaḥ |27||

He who is Rudra is verily God; He is the subtle, [and] prostrations to Him again and again.

2.28 यो वै रुद्रः स भगवान् यच्च शुक्लं तस्मै वै नमो नमः ।२८॥

Yo vai Rudraḥ sa bhagavān yacca śuklaṁ tasmai vai namo namaḥ |28||

He who is Rudra is verily God; He is the white (or pure), [and] prostrations to Him again and again.

2.29 यो वै रुद्रः स भगवान् यच्च कृष्णं तस्मै वै नमो नमः ।२९॥

Yo vai Rudraḥ sa bhagavān yacca kṛṣṇaṁ tasmai vai namo namaḥ |29||

He who is Rudra is verily God; He is the black, [and] prostrations to Him again and again.

2.30 [1]**यो वै रुद्रः स भगवान् यच्च कृत्स्नं तस्मै वै नमो नमः |३०||**

Yo vai Rudraḥ sa bhagavān yacca kṛtsnaṁ tasmai vai namo namaḥ |30||

> He who is Rudra is verily God; He is everything, [and] prostrations to Him again and again.

2.31 यो वै रुद्रः स भगवान् यच्च सत्यं तस्मै वै नमो नमः |३१||

Yo vai Rudraḥ sa bhagavān yacca satyaṁ tasmai vai namo namaḥ |31||

> He who is Rudra is verily God; He is the Truth, [and] prostrations to Him again and again.

2.32 यो वै रुद्रः स भगवान् यच्च सर्वं तस्मै वै नमो नमः |३२|| || २ ||

Yo vai Rudraḥ sa bhagavān yacca sarvaṁ tasmai vai namo namaḥ |32||2||

---

[1]विश्वं कृत्स्नं जगत्सर्वं सत्यं तस्मै नमो नमः || Liṅga II.18.3
Viśvaṁ kṛtsnaṁ jagat-sarvaṁ satyaṁ tasmai namo-namaḥ ||

> He who is Rudra is verily God; He is all, [and] prostrations to Him again and again.

Thus, based on Mantra 2, we can say that the whole world is a manifestation of Rudra, who is not different from *Brahman* – *Sarvaṁ khalvidaṁ Brahma*; all this is indeed *Brahman*.

|| Thus, ends Mantra 2 ||

||  ||

Mantra 3

The glorification of Rudra continues. Rudra or *Brahman*, who is one, manifests as the world. At the time of dissolution, He devours everything, and then everything goes back to Him. Because of His various roles, Rudra has been given many epithets.

3.1a भूस्ते आदिर्मध्यं भुवस्ते स्वस्ते शीर्षं विश्वरूपोऽसि –
Bhūste ādir-madhyaṁ bhuvaste svaste śīrṣaṁ viśvarūpo'si –

> [O Rudra,] the earth is Your lower part (or feet), the mid-region (the space between earth and heaven) is Your middle part, and the heaven is Your head; You have appeared as this world.

The world is Rudra's body; it is His manifestation.

3.1b [1]ब्रह्मैकस्त्वं द्विधा त्रिधा वृद्धिस्त्वं शान्तिस्त्वं पुष्टिस्त्वं –

---

[1]ब्रह्मैकस्त्वं द्वित्रिधार्थमधश्च त्वं सुरेश्वरः । Liṅga II.18.5
Brahmaikas-tvaṁ dvi-tridhārtha-madhaśca tvaṁ sureśvaraḥ |

brahmaikastvaṁ dvidhā tridhā vṛddhistvaṁ śāntistvaṁ puṣṭistvaṁ –

> As *Brahman* (the Absolute Reality), You are one, [as manifest and un-manifest] You appear as two, [as *Bhuḥ*, *Bhuvaḥ*, *Svaḥ*] You are seen as three, [as this universe] You manifest as multi-formed; You are tranquility; You are nourishment.

Dvidhā – It means twofold; as 'manifest and un-manifest' world, He is twofold. Before the existence of the world, only *Brahman* existed. Then, *Brahman* thought, 'I am one, let me be many – *Eko'haṁ bahu syām* (एकोऽहं बहु स्याम्).' Thus, unmanifest *Brahman* became the manifest universe, and therefore, became two.

Tridhā – It means three-fold. *Bhuḥ*, *Bhuvaḥ*, and *Svaḥ* – the three worlds (*Lokas*) are his manifestation (see the commentary on Mantra 2.14).

Vṛddhiḥ – It means increase. From being one *Brahman*, He has become many – people, animals, birds, planets, stars, galaxies, super galaxies, a cluster of galaxies, black holes, black material, black energy, etc. The ever-expanding universe is the manifestation of *Brahman*.

3.1c हुतमहुतं दत्तमदत्तं सर्वमसर्वं विश्वमविश्वं कृतमकृतं परमपरं परायणञ्च त्वम् ।

Hutama-hutaṁ dattama-dattaṁ sarvama-sarvaṁ viśvama-viśvaṁ kṛtama-kṛtaṁ prarama-paraṁ parāyañca tvam |

> You are the oblation and no-oblation; You are the charity as well as no charity. You are everything, [and at the same time] You are nothing, You are this world as well as no-world. You are the good deed that is done as well as not done; You are the supreme as well as that which is not supreme. You are the refuge [of all].

Hutamahutam (*hutaṁ-ahutam*) – the act of pouring the material of offerings (*havi*) in the sacrificial fire (*yajña* - यज्ञ, *homam* or *havan*) is called '*hutam.*' *Ahutam* means, 'that which is not offered.' It is all *Brahman*, whether it is offered in the sacrificial fire or not. The *Bhagavad Gītā* IV.24 says:

ब्रह्मार्पणं ब्रह्म हविर्ब्रह्माग्नौ ब्रह्मणा हुतम् |
ब्रह्मैव तेन गन्तव्यं ब्रह्मकर्मसमाधिना ||

Brahmārpaṇaṁ Brahma havir-
Brahmāgnau brahmaṇāhutam |
Brahmaiva tena gantavyaṁ
Brahma – karma - samādhinā ||

> The ladle [with which one pours the material of oblation] is *Brahman*, the material of oblation is *Brahman*, the [sacrificial] fire [in which the material is poured] is *Brahman*, the

> act of offering by the Brahmin [who too is *Brahman*] is *Brahman*, and *Brahman* indeed is the goal to be attained by the one who is absorbed in the [sacrificial] act, which is *Brahman.*

Paramaparam – *Paraṁ-Aparam*: *Param* or *Para* means higher, supreme, beyond (transcendental), or at a far distance. *Aparam* is the opposite of *param*. Rudra is Supreme, beyond or transcendent, and too far away. He is also not supreme, meaning He is mundane; he is very near.

Parāyaṇa – It means the last resort or refuge. Rudra or *Brahman* is the refuge of all.

The *Upaniṣads* proclaim, 'All this indeed is *Brahman*.' *Śrīmad Bhagavad-Gītā* (VII.19) says the same thing 'all is *Vāsudeva Śrī Kṛṣṇa* (God) – *Vāsudevaḥ sarvam* (वासुदेवः सर्वम्).'

3.2 [1]**अपाम सोमममृता अभूमागन्म ज्योतिरविदाम देवान् । किं नूनमस्मान् कृणवदरातिः किमु धूर्तिरमृतं मर्त्यस्य ।**

Apāma somama-mṛtā abhūmāganma jyotira-vidāma devān | Kiṁ nūna-masmān kṛṇa-vadarātiḥ kimu dhūrti-ramṛtaṁ martyasya |

> We drank the soma juice (meaning, the nectar of Your grace) and became immortal, attained

---

[1]*Ṛgveda* XIII.48.3 and the *Liṅga Purāṇa* II.18.7 give the same hymn.

> the light (meaning, the divine wisdom), and came to know the divine beings (gods).
>
> You are the nectar (ambrosia) of immortality for a mortal; [when Your grace is with us,] how indeed can an enemy give us pain and cause us any injury?

Apāma somam – It means we drank Soma. *Soma* is a divine juice equivalent to nectar (*amṛta*), which gives immortality.

Amṛtā abhūma – *Amṛtāḥ abhūma*: It means we became immortal.

Āganma jyotiḥ – It means attained the light, i.e., divine knowledge or wisdom.

Vidāma devān – It means we have known the gods (*devas*).

Kiṁ nūnamasmān kṛṇavad – *Kiṁ nūnaṁ asmān kṛṇavat*: It means, 'what can he indeed do to us?'

Arātiḥ – Enemy; *Dhūrti* – Injury; *Martyasya* – of a mortal.

3.3 सोमसूर्यपुरस्तात् सूक्ष्मः पुरुषः ।

Soma-sūrya-purastāt sūkṣmaḥ puruṣaḥ |

> You are the subtle Being, more ancient than the sun and the moon.

3.4 [1]सर्वं जगद्धितं वा एतदक्षरं प्राजापत्यं सौम्यं सूक्ष्मं पुरुषं ग्राह्यमग्राह्येण भावं भावेन सौम्यं सौम्येन सूक्ष्मं सूक्ष्मेण वायव्यं वायव्येन ग्रसति तस्मै महाग्रासाय वै नमो नमः ।

Sarvaṁ jagaddhitaṁ vā etadakṣaraṁ prājāpatyaṁ saumyaṁ sūkṣmaṁ puruṣaṁ grāhya-magrāhyeṇa bhāvaṁ bhāvena saumyaṁ saumyena sūkṣmaṁ sūkṣmeṇa vāyavyaṁ vāyavyena grasati tasmai mahā-grāsāya vai namo namaḥ |

Again, and again, obeisance to Him, the Great Devourer, this (ancient) imperishable, serene, and subtle Being (*Puruṣa*) who is indeed beneficent to the whole world created by *Prajāpati* (*Brahmā*). He devours perceptible objects with imperceptible ones, feelings with feelings, serene with serene, subtle with subtle, and vital airs with vital airs.

---

[1]एतज्जगद्धितं दिव्यमक्षरं सूक्ष्ममव्ययम् ॥ Liṅga II.18.8
Etaj-jagad-dhitaṁ divya-makṣaraṁ sūkṣma-mavyayam ||

प्राजापत्यं पवित्रं च सौम्यमग्राह्यमव्ययम् । Liṅga II.18.9
Prājāpatyatṁ pavitraṁ ca saumya-magrāhya-mavyayam |

सौम्येन सौम्यं ग्रसति तेजसा स्वेन लीलया ।
तस्मै नमोऽपसंहर्त्रे महाग्रासाय शूलिने ॥ Liṅga II.18.10
Saumyena saumyaṁ grasati tejasā svena līlayā |
Tasmai namo'pa-saṁhartre mahāgrāsāya Śūline ||

Sarvaṁ jagaddhitam – *Sarvaṁ jagat-hitam*: It means 'to the one who is beneficent to the whole world'.

Everything is Rudra or *Brahman's* manifestation. Rudra as *Brahmā* creates the world and as *Viṣṇu* preserves it and takes care of it, and therefore, He is described as beneficent.

Puruṣa – Here, *Puruṣa*, which I have translated as Being, refers to Rudra, who is imperishable (*akṣaram*), serene (*saumyam*), and subtle (*sūkṣmam*).

Grāhya – one who (or which) can be grabbed or comprehended, meaning perceptible.

Agrāhya – It means one who (or which) cannot be seized or captured, or in other words, cannot be comprehended or perceived; i.e., imperceptible. Rudra or *Brahman* cannot be comprehended by sense organs, mind, and intellect, and therefore, He is *agrāhya*.

Sense organs can perceive the objects of the world, but they cannot perceive the mind; therefore, the mind is *agrāhya* for the sense organs. The mind cannot understand the intellect, and therefore, the intellect is *agrāhya* for the mind. The intellect cannot comprehend the *Ātman*, the Self within; and thus, the *Ātman* is *agrāhya* for the intellect. Being the *Ātman* of all living beings, *Brahman* is *agrāhya* (imperceptible) to all.

Bhāva – feeling, sentiment, emotion, intuition, or intent. It also means existence.

Saumya – gentle, auspicious, or serene. The literal meaning of the word *saumya* is anything related to soma, meaning the moon. Being cool, auspicious, and serene are the qualities of the moon.

Sūkṣma – subtle.

Vāyavya – It means a thing which has come forth from *Vāyu* (the wind or air) or the one which is related to *Vāyu.* Based on this meaning, I have translated *Vāyavya* as vital airs, meaning *Prāṇas*. There are five *Prāṇas* – *Prāṇa*, *Apāna*, *Vyāna*, *Udāna*, and *Samāna*. These are the vital airs or energies in our body that keep our body and mind healthy and functioning. For more details, see the Mantra 4.1 commentary.

Vāyavya is also the name of a utensil, which looks like a mortar, that is used for *yajña* (यज्ञ - holy fire) ceremony. Its other meaning is the north-west corner of the *Yajña* altar; *Vāyu* is its presiding deity.

Mahā-grāsāya – for the great devourer or swallower.

At the time of dissolution (*pralaya*) of the world, everything dissolves back into *Brahman*. Personal feelings, serenity, subtlety, and vital airs get dissolved in cosmic feelings, serenity, subtlety, and vital airs respectively, and then the whole cosmos gets absorbed in the Primordial Nature (*Mūla-Prakṛti* - मूलप्रकृति). Finally, the Primordial Nature gets absorbed in Rudra or *Brahman*. It could be said that Rudra devours or swallows all, and therefore, he is called the Great Devourer.

3.5 [1]**हृदिस्था देवता: सर्वा हृदि प्राणा: प्रतिष्ठिता: । हृदि त्वमसि यो नित्यं तिस्रो मात्रा: परस्तु स: ।**

Hṛdisthā devatāḥ sarvā hṛdi prāṇāḥ pratiṣṭhitāḥ |
Hṛdi tvamasi yo nityaṁ tisro mātrāḥ parastu saḥ |

> All the gods and the vital airs (*Prāṇas*) are stationed in the heart. You too always dwell within the heart in the form of the three *mātrās*; however, You indeed are beyond them.

The last part of the text – *parastu saḥ* – addresses to Rudra in the third person as *saḥ*, meaning 'He,' which I have translated as 'You' to maintain the continuity in the sentence.

Three *mātrās* (मात्रा): *Mātrās* are syllables or letters. The three *mātrās* refer to the three constituting letters of the word OM (ओम्) – *A*, *U*, and *M* (अ, उ, म्). According to the Sanskrit grammar, when *U* (उ) follows *A* (अ), both together become *O* (ओ); thus, *A+U+M* becomes OM. Om is also written as a symbol ॐ. Whether one writes OM as symbol ॐ or OM or AUM, it must be pronounced as OM as in h***om***e or d***om***e.

Though the gods, vital airs, and Rudra too reside in the heart, Rudra or *Brahman* is beyond gods and vital airs.

---

[1] हृदिस्था देवता: सर्वा हृदि प्राणे प्रतिष्ठिता: ।
हृदि त्वमसि यो नित्यं तिस्रो मात्रा: परस्तु स: ॥ Liṅga II.18.11
Hṛdisthā devatāḥ sarvā hṛdi prāṇe pratiṣṭhitāḥ |
Hṛdi tvamasi yo nityaṁ tisro mātrāḥ parastu saḥ ||

The three *mātrās A*, *U*, and *M* represent the three states of waking, dreaming, and deep sleep, respectively. Rudra transcends these three states of existence.

Rudra is another name of *Brahman*; thus, Om represents Rudra. Since the three *mātrās A*, *U*, *M* are only parts of the word OM, and OM represents Rudra, he is undoubtedly superior to the three *mātrās*, and hence, He transcends the three *mātrās*.

For further details and significance of OM and the three *mātrās*, see the commentary on Mantra 5.5.

3.6 [1]**तस्योत्तरतः शिरो दक्षिणतः पादौ य उत्तरतः स ओङ्कारः य ओङ्कारः स प्रणवः यः प्रणवः स सर्वव्यापी यः सर्वव्यापी सोऽनन्तः योऽनन्तस्तत्तारं यत्तारं तच्छुक्लं यच्छुक्लं तत्सूक्ष्मं यत्सूक्ष्मं तद्वैद्युतं यद्वैद्युतं तत्परं ब्रह्म यत्परं ब्रह्म स**

---

[1] शिरश्चोत्तरतश्चैव पादौ दक्षिणस्तथा ।
यो वै चोत्तरतः साक्षात्स ओङ्कारः सनातनः ॥ Liṅga II.18.12
Śiraścottarataś-caiva pādau dakṣiṇas-tathā |
Yo vai cottarataḥ sākṣāt-sa Oṅkāraḥ sanātanaḥ ||

ओङ्कारो यः स एवेह प्रणवो व्याप्य तिष्ठति ।
अनन्तस्तारसूक्ष्मं च शुक्लं वैद्युतमेव च ॥ Liṅga II.18.13
Oṅkāro yaḥ sa eveha praṇavo vyāpya tiṣṭhati |
Anantastāra-sūkṣmaṁ ca śuklaṁ vaidyutameva ca ||

परं ब्रह्म स ईशान एको रुद्रः स एव च ।
भवान्महेश्वरः साक्षान्महादेवो न संशयः ॥ Liṅga II.18.14
Paraṁ Brahma sa Īśāna eko Rudraḥ sa eva ca |
Bhavān Maheśvaraḥ sākṣān Mahādevo na saṁśayaḥ ||

एकः य एकः स रुद्रः यो रुद्रः स ईशानः य ईशानः स भगवान् महेश्वरः ॥ ३ ॥

Tasyottarataḥ śiro dakṣiṇataḥ pādau ya uttarataḥ sa oṅkāraḥ ya oṅkāraḥ sa praṇavaḥ yaḥ praṇavaḥ sa sarvavyāpī yaḥ sarvavyāpī so'nantaḥ yo'nantas-tat-tāraṁ yat-tāraṁ tac-chuklaṁ yac-chuklaṁ tat sūkṣmaṁ yat sūkṣmaṁ tad-vaidyutaṁ yad-vaidyutaṁ tat paraṁ Brahma yat paraṁ Brahma sa ekaḥ ya ekaḥ sa Rudraḥ yo Rudraḥ sa Īśānaḥ ya Īśānaḥ sa bhagavān Maheśvaraḥ ||3||

> His head is towards the north, and the feet are towards the south. The One who is in the north is *Oṅkāra*, *Oṅkāra* is *Praṇava. Praṇava* is all-pervading, and the all-pervading is infinite. The infinite is the Savior, who is pure. The pure One is subtle, and the subtle One is the flash of lightning. The flash of lightning is the Supreme *Brahman*, who is One (i.e., *Brahman* alone exists). That who is One is Rudra, Rudra is *Īśāna*, and *Īśāna* is Lord *Maheśvara*.

Oṅkāra – *Oṅkāra* (or *Oṁkāra*), Om, symbol ॐ, and *Praṇava* are synonymous. Since Om is another name of *Brahman* – who is all-pervading – *Praṇava* too is all-pervading.

Ananta – It means one who has neither a beginning nor an end, i.e., infinite.

Tāra – It means one who carries across, i.e., Savior. In Indian spirituality, the world is compared with an ocean; it is Rudra who takes His devotees across the ocean of the world, meaning He gives them emancipation.

Śukla – *Śukla* means white or pure.

Rudra, *Īśāna*, and *Maheśvara* are some of the names of Lord Śiva.

|| Thus, ends Mantra 3 ||

||  ||

Mantra 4

In Mantra 3, Rudra is addressed by so many epithets – *Oṅkāra*, *Praṇava*, *Sarvavyāpī*, *Ananta*, *Tāra*, *Śukla*, *Sūkṣma*, *Vaidyuta*, *Brahma*, *Eka*, Rudra, *Īśana*, and *Bhagavān Maheśvara.* Mantra 4 explains why He is called by these names.

4.1 [1]अथ कस्मादुच्यते ओङ्कारः । यस्मादुच्चार्यमाण एव प्राणानूर्ध्वमुत्क्रामयति तस्मादुच्यते ओङ्कारः ।

Atha kasmāducyate Oṅkāraḥ | *Yasmā-duccārya-māṇa eva prāṇā-nūrdhva-mut-krāmayati tasmāducyate Oṅkāraḥ* |

> Why is He called *Oṅkāra* (or *Oṁkāra*)? He is called *Oṅkāra* or the sound Om because, with a mere recitation of Om, He uplifts the vital airs (*Prāṇas*).

Uccārya-māṇa eva prāṇān ūrdhvaṁ utkrāmayati – It means, its simple utterance moves the breath upwards. *Utkram* means

---

[1] ऊर्ध्वमुन्नामयत्येव स ओङ्कारः प्रकीर्तितः । Liṅga II.18.15
Ūrdhvamun-nāmayatyeva sa Oṅkāraḥ prakīrtitaḥ |

to ascend; *utkrāmayati* is its causative case. When you say the word Om, you will feel your breath moving upwards.

A simple meaning of the word *Prāṇa* is breath; however, it has a deeper meaning. *Prāṇa* is a vital energy in the body; it is not just breath. By breathing air in and out through respiration, we supply energy to our body, which nourishes and maintains the functioning of our body, mind, and intellect. *Prāṇa* is further divided into five categories based on its activity. There are five *Prāṇas* (*Pañca-Prāṇa* पञ्चप्राण) – *Prāṇa*, *Apāna*, *Vyāna*, *Udāna*, and *Samāna*.

- *Prāṇa* (प्राण) – *Prāṇa* is the energy due to which one can breathe. It is located in the heart. It is a sign of life; if a person cannot breathe, he is considered dead. Of course, with the help of machines, you can forcibly keep a person alive, but as soon you disconnect the devices, and if he cannot breathe naturally, he is dead.

- *Apāna* (अपान) – This vital energy flows downwards and helps in excreting the waste, and thus, it keeps a person healthy.

- *Vyāna* (व्यान) – This energy flows all around the body. It is this energy due to which our nerves, arteries, and veins work.

- *Udāna* (उदान) – This vital air is located in the throat. Tears and vomiting are due to this energy. When a person's stomach is upset, he throws up, and after throwing up, he feels temporarily better. Also, at the time of death, it is *Udāna* energy, which takes the *Jivātman* (soul) to other regions.

- *Samāna* (समान) – This vital air is located in the navel and helps in digesting food.

Here is a verse which tells us the locations of the five vital airs:

हृदि प्राणो गुदेऽपानः समानो नाभिमण्डले ।
उदानः कण्ठनालेषु व्यानः सर्वशरीरगः ॥

Hṛdi prāṇo gude'pānaḥ samāno nābhimaṇḍale |
Udānaḥ kaṇṭha-nāleṣu vyānaḥ sarva-śarīragaḥ ||

> *Prāṇa*, *Apāna*, *Samāna*, *Udāna*, and *Vyāna* are respectively located in the heart, the organ of excretion, area of navel, throat, and all over the body.

Om is a powerful mantra. By uttering Om, a person is revitalizing his energies, which keeps him healthy. When a person repeats Om again and again (meaning, doing *japa* जप), not only he energizes his body by uplifting his *prāṇas* but also quietens his mind and thus uplifts himself spiritually. The *Liṅga Purāṇa* II.18, Verse 15 confirms this: The one who elevates or helps move upwards is known as *Oṅkāra* – *Ūrdhvaṁ unnāmayati eva saḥ Oṅkāraḥ prakīrtitaḥ* (ऊर्ध्वं उन्नामयति एव सः ओंकारः प्रकीर्तितः).

4.2 [1]अथ कस्मादुच्यते प्रणवः यस्मादुच्चार्यमाण एव ऋग्यजुःसामाथर्वाङ्गिरसं ब्रह्म ब्राह्मणेभ्यः प्रणामयति नामयति च तस्मादुच्यते प्रणवः ।

Atha kasmāducyate praṇavaḥ yasmā-duccāryamāṇa eva Ṛg-Yajuḥ-Sāmā-tharvāṅgi-rasaṁ Brahma brāhmaṇebhyaḥ praṇāmayati nāmayati ca tasmā-ducyate praṇavaḥ |

> Why is He called *Praṇava*? He is called *Praṇava* because its mere recitation makes *Ṛgveda*, *Yajurveda*, *Sāmaveda, Atharvaveda, Añgirasa* (an ancient sage who was a seer of *Vedas*), and *Brahmā* (the creator) to bow down to *Brahmins* (priests).

In this mantra, the meaning of the word *praṇāmayati* (प्रणामयति) is further emphasized as *nāmayati* (नामयति), both have the same definition. Grammatically, they are causative verbs, and mean 'makes someone prostrate or bow down.' *Praṇava* (प्रणव) or Om is a very sacred and powerful mantra. When Brahmins (Hindu priests) recite Vedas, they utter Om before every mantra. Just uttering Om makes Brahmins pure, and noble of respect and adoration. They become so worthy that even *Ṛgveda*, *Yajurveda*, *Sāmaveda*, *Atharvaveda*,

---

[1] प्राणानवति यस्तस्मात्प्रणवः परिकीर्तितः ॥ Linga II.18.15
Prāṇānavati yastasmāt praṇavaḥ parikīrtitaḥ ||

Aṅgirasa, and *Brahmā* bow down to the Brahmins who chant Om.

Such Brahmin must possess the qualities as explained in the commentary on Mantra 1.3i. It is also said: 'One who knows *Brahman* is a Brahmin – *Brahma jānāti brāhmaṇaḥ* (ब्रह्म जानाति ब्राह्मण:)'.

The *Śiva-Mahā-Purāṇa*, *Kailāsa Saṁhitā* (शिवमहापुराण, कैलास संहिता), Chapter 3 glorifies *Praṇava* as such: There is no difference between Lord Śiva (Rudra), who is *Brahman*, and *Praṇava* (Verse 7). Om is called *Praṇava* because it is *Prāṇa*, the life-energy, of all – from *Brahmā*, the creator, down to all living beings (Verse 14).

4.3 [1]**अथ कस्मादुच्यते सर्वव्यापी यस्मादुच्चार्यमाण एव यथा स्नेहेन पललपिण्डमिव शान्तरूपमोतप्रोतमनुप्राप्तो व्यतिषक्तश्च तस्मादुच्यते सर्वव्यापी ।**

Atha kasmāducyate sarvavyāpī yasmā-duccārya-māṇa eva yathā snehena palala-piṇḍamiva śantarūpa-motaprota-manuprāpto vyatiṣaktaśca tasmā-duccyate sarvavyāpī |

> Why is He called all-pervading? It is like oil, which is spread all over in a lump of ground sesame. When His name is chanted, He quietly

---

[1] सर्वं व्याप्नोति यस्मात्सर्वव्यापी सनातन: | Liṅga II.18.16
Sarvaṁ vyāpnoti yasmāt sarvavyāpī sanātanaḥ |

pervades all surroundings with His presence and intermingles with them (meaning permeates them), without being noticed [by the aspirant]; therefore, He is called all-pervading.

Sneha – oil; *Vyatiṣakta* – intertwined

Otaprota-manuprāpto – *Otaprotaṁ anuprāptaḥ*: *Otaprota* means sewn lengthwise and crosswise, and *anuprāptaḥ* means one who has reached or arrived. Thus, the phrase means He pervades all surroundings (all directions, length and breadthwise).

Palalapiṇḍamiva – *Palalapiṇḍaṁ iva*: It means like a lump of ground sesame seeds. When sesame seeds are ground, there is oil all over, inside as well outside.

4.4 अथ कस्मादुच्यतेऽनन्तः । यस्मादुच्चार्यमाण एव तिर्यगूर्ध्वमधस्ताच्चास्यान्तो नोपलभ्यते तस्मा-दुच्यतेऽनन्तः ।

Atha kasmā-ducyate'nantaḥ | Yasmā-duccārya-māṇa eva tiryagūrdhva-madhastāc-cāsyānto nopalabhyate tasmā-ducyate'nantaḥ |

Why is He called infinite? He is called infinite because when his name is chanted, His beginning, as well as the end, cannot be found either upwards, downwards, or sideways.

Tiryagūrdhva-madhastāt – It means from sideways, above, and below.

When a seeker recites Lord Śiva's name with devotion and faith, he goes to a meditative state and realizes that it is all Śiva, in all directions, having neither a beginning nor an end; the duality disappears.

4.5 [1]अथ कस्मादुच्यते तारं यस्मादुच्चार्यमाण एव गर्भजन्म-व्याधिजरामरणसंसार-महाभयात् तारयति त्रायते च तस्मादुच्यते तारम् ।

Atha kasmāducyate tāraṁ yasmā-duccārya-māṇa eva garbha-janma-vyādhi-jarā-maraṇa-saṁsāra-mahā-bhayāt tārayati trāyate ca tasmāducyate tāram |

> Why is He called Savior? He is called Savior because when His name is recited, He helps [His devotees] to cross the [ocean of] *saṁsāra* (meaning, the world) and protects them from the greatest fear – the fear of being conceived and born, and [then suffering due to] disease, old age, and death.

The *Sanātana* Dharma (Hindu) philosophy believes that the *Jīva* (individual soul – the embodied and conditioned self)

---

[1] यस्तारयति संसारात्तार इत्यभिधीयते ॥ Liṅga II.18.17
Yas tārayati saṁsārāt tāra ityabhidhīyate ||

goes through various phases – first, he is conceived in a womb, then takes birth, suffers due to disease and old age, and finally, he faces death (death of the body), and once again he reincarnates. Thus, the cycle of births and deaths goes on until the *Jīva* is liberated. This world is called *Saṁsāra*, where *Jīva* comes and goes. The world is compared with the ocean; crossing the ocean means stopping the process of births and deaths and getting liberated.

Tāra or *Tāraka*, *Tārayati*, and *Trāyate* – The word *Tāra* or *Tāraka* is a noun, and it means 'one who helps to cross [the ocean],' or in other words, it means 'Savior.' The term *Tārayati* is a verb, and it means 'helps to cross.' *Trāyate* is a verb meaning 'protects.' Rudra or Lord Śiva protects His devotees. It is only due to Lord Śiva's grace that one can cross the ocean of the world – the cycle of repeated births and deaths – and be free.

4.6 अथ कस्मादुच्यते शुक्लं यस्मादुच्चार्यमाण एव क्लन्दते क्लामयति च तस्मादुच्यते शुक्लम् ।

Atha kasmāducyate śuklaṁ yasmā-duccārya-māṇa eva klandate klāmayati ca tasmāducyate śuklam |

> Why is He called *Śukla* (or pure)? He is called *Śukla* because when His name is uttered, He grieves [on seeing His devotees suffering], and makes [their miseries and pains] end.

Klandate – It means He is troubled, or He grieves.

Klāmayati – *Klam* means to get exhausted, and *Klāmayati* means He makes [something] to exhaust or end.

Śukla – The word *Śukla* means white, pure, or unsullied. *Śukla* is made up of two words – *śu* + *kla*. The meaning of *śu* (शु) is quickly or swiftly, and according to this mantra, *kla* (क्ल) stands for *kland* (to grieve) and *klam* (to become exhausted). Thus, *Śukla* is the one who grieves [to see the sufferings of devotees] and swiftly makes [their miseries] to exhaust.

One of the Lord Śiva's names is *Āśutoṣa* (आशुतोष), meaning one who is pleased quickly. Why is He satisfied so fast? Because He is *Śukla* – pure and soft-hearted. He cries when His devotees suffer; devotees' pain is His pain. That is why the mantra uses the word *klandate*, meaning He grieves. He is called Rudra because He cries (*rodati* - रोदति) when His devotees go through miseries.

When Lord Śiva sees His devotees suffering, what else does He do in addition to crying? *Klāmayati*. Grammatically, *klāmayati* is the causative of verb *klam*. Thus, *klāmayati* means 'to cause to exhaust' – He causes miseries of the devotees to exhaust or end.

Each action has a reaction. According to the Law of Karma, Good deeds lead to a comfortable life, whereas bad actions result in suffering. Joys and sorrows are the results of the past karmas. Until the past karmas are exhausted by experiencing (*bhoga* - भोग) their consequences, a person remains bonded and cannot be free from the cycle of births and deaths.

However, when Lord Śiva is pleased due to the devotion and austerity of a person, He washes off all his karmas, virtuous as well as bad, and makes his karmas exhaust (*klāmayati*). As a result, the person is free, and there are no more births and deaths for him.

The concept that Lord Śiva destroys all the past karmas is based on the dualistic theory – Śiva is different from the devotee; *Brahman* and *Ātman* are different from one another. If we look at it from the Vedantic or non-dualistic point of view, Lord Śiva – *Brahman* – dwells within all living beings as their *Ātman*, the Self. When the aspirant meditates on Lord Śiva, in fact, he is meditating on his Inner Self, the *Ātman*. All his senses, mind, intellect, and ego, all merge with his Inner Self, he loses his worldly identity and becomes one with the Cosmic Self – Śiva or *Brahman*. It is the actual experience of spiritual knowledge (*Tattva-Jñāna* - तत्त्वज्ञान), which burns all the past karmas. Lord *Śrī Kṛṣṇa* says in the *Bhagavad-Gītā* (IV.37), "O Arjuna, the fire of spiritual knowledge burns all the karmas the way regular fire burns the wood."

4.7 [1]**अथ कस्मादुच्यते सूक्ष्मं यस्मादुच्चार्यमाण एव सूक्ष्मो भूत्वा शरीराण्यधितिष्ठति सर्वाणि चाङ्गान्यभिमृश्यति तस्मादुच्यते सूक्ष्मम् ।**

---

[1] सूक्ष्मो भूत्वा शरीराणि सर्वदा ह्यधितिष्ठति ।
तस्मात्सूक्ष्मः समाख्यातो भगवान्नीललोहितः ॥ Linga II.18.18
Sūkṣmo bhūtvā śarīrāṇi sarvadā hyadhi-tiṣṭhati |
Tasmāt sūkṣmaḥ samākhyāto bhagavān nīlalohitaḥ ||

Atha kasmāducyate sūkṣmaṁ yasmā-duccārya-māṇa eva sūkṣmo bhūtvā śarīrāṇyadhi-tiṣṭhati sarvāṇi cāṅgānyabhi-mṛśyati tasmāducyate sūkṣmam |

> Why is He called subtle? He is called subtle because, when His name is chanted, He, by taking a subtle form, inhabits all bodies, and touches [and pervades] all limbs.

Adhitiṣṭhati – He inhabits or stands upon; *Abhimṛśyati* – He touches.

When a devotee chants Lord Śiva's name and meditates on Him, he feels bliss in his heart as well as in all his limbs. This bliss is part of the supreme Bliss of Lord Śiva, who is *Sat-Cit-Ānand* – Existence-Consciousness-Bliss. During meditation, when the aspirant feels thrilled due to joy, his limbs shiver due to ecstasy, it is because Lord Śiva manifests in the body of the aspirant; Lord Śiva lovingly touches his body. Each cell of the body rejoices and gets invigorated.

4.8 अथ कस्मादुच्यते वैद्युतम् । यस्मादुच्चार्यमाण एव व्यक्ते महति तमसि द्योतयति तस्मादुच्यते वैद्युतम् ।

Atha kasmāducyate vaidyutam | *Yasmā-duccārya-māṇa eva vyakte mahati tamasi dyotayati tasmā-ducyate vaidyutam* |

> Why is He called radiant? He is called radiant because when His name is chanted, He removes the extreme darkness [of ignorance

> from the hearts of the aspirants] and illumines them [with the light of *jñāna* – the spiritual knowledge].

Vyakte – in manifested [objects]; *Vaidyuta* – brilliant, the fire of lightning, or radiant; *Dyotayati* – He illumines.

Mahati tamasi – It means in extreme darkness. Darkness refers to ignorance (*ajñāna* अज्ञान) – the absence of spirituality or spiritual knowledge.

If we go by the literal meaning of the mantra, it says, "Why is He called radiant? He is called radiant because He illumines all the manifested objects surrounded by the extreme darkness." All the stars in galaxies are shining because of the radiance of Lord Śiva.

4.9 [1]**अथ कस्मादुच्यते परं ब्रह्म यस्मात् परमपरं परायणञ्च बृहद्-बृहत्या बृंहयति तस्मादुच्यते परं ब्रह्म ।**

Atha kasmāducyate parāṁ Brahma yasmāt parama-paraṁ parāyaṇañca bṛhad-bṛhatyā bṛṁhayati tasmā-ducyate paraṁ Brahma |

> Why is He called Supreme *Brahman*? He is the greatest of the greatest; He is the refuge of all. He is infinite; with His quality of being

[1] बृहत्त्वाद्-बृहणत्वाच्च बृहते च परापरे ॥ Linga II.18.20
तस्माद्-बृंहति यस्माद्धि परं ब्रह्मेति कीर्तितम् । Linga II.18.21
Bṛhattvād-bṛhaṇatvāc-ca bṛhate ca parāpare ||
Tasmād-bṛṁhati yasmāddhi paraṁ brahmeti kīrtitam |

limitless and making others vast, He causes others to expand (meaning evolve). That is why He is called the Supreme *Brahman*.

Parama-param – *Parama* means the highest, best, most excellent, higher than, superior to. *Param* means beyond or greatly. *Paramaparam* means the highest of the highest.

Parāyaṇa – The word *parāyaṇa* is made up of two words, *para* (supreme) + *ayana* (abode or resort). Thus, *Parāyaṇa* means supreme abode or supreme resort or refuge. *Brahman* or Lord Śiva is the refuge of all. In the *Bhagavad Gītā* X.12, *Arjuna* addresses Lord *Kṛṣṇa* as '*Paraṁ Brahma Paraṁ Dhāma;*' *dhāma* means abode.

Bṛh or *bṛṁh* – to increase or expand.

Bṛhat, bṛhatyā – these words are derived from the root word *Bṛh* (बृह्). *Bṛhat* (बृहत्) means vast (or infinite) or extended; *bṛhatyā* (बृहत्या) means because of His quality of being vast;

Bṛṁhayati – it is derived from the verb *bṛṁh*; *bṛṁhayati* (बृंहयति) means He makes others expand.

Brahma – the word *Brahma* or *Brahman* is derived from the Sanskrit root word *bṛh*, meaning to increase or expand. *Bṛhattvāt Brahma gīyate* (बृहत्त्वात् ब्रह्म गीयते) – he is called *Brahma* because he expands. The universe is called *brahmāṇḍa* (ब्रह्माण्ड), literally meaning the egg of *Brahman*. According to astrophysics, the universe is expanding at an accelerated rate; galaxies are moving away from one another. Therefore, *brahmāṇḍa* is a very appropriate term for the world. *Brahman* or *Brahma* (the Absolute Reality or Absolute God) is the one who makes the universe expand further and further. The Ultimate Reality (*Brahman*) is Supreme, whereas the world (*brahmāṇḍa*) is not supreme, even though it is a manifestation of *Brahman*.

4.10 अथ कस्मादुच्यते एकः यः सर्वान् प्राणान् सम्भक्ष्य सम्भक्षणेनाजः संसृजति विसृजति तीर्थमेके व्रजन्ति तीर्थमेके दक्षिणाः प्रत्यञ्च उदञ्चः प्राञ्चोऽभिव्रजन्त्येके तेषां सर्वेषामिह सङ्गतिः साकं स [1]एकोऽभूदन्तश्चरति प्रजानां तस्मादुच्यते एकः ।

Atha kasmāducyate ekaḥ yaḥ sarvān prāṇān saṁbhakṣya saṁ-bhakṣaṇenājaḥ saṁsṛjati visṛjati tīrthameke vrajanti tīrthameke dakṣināḥ pratyañca udañcaḥ prāñco'bhi-vrajantyeke teṣāṁ sarveṣāmiha saṅgatiḥ sākaṁ sa [2]*eko'bhūdantaś-carati prajānāṁ tasmāducyate ekaḥ* |

> Why is He called One? He, the unborn, [who alone existed before the creation], devours all lives, then He creates [them back] and destroys [them again]. Some go for pilgrimage to the holy places – some to the south and some to the west, north or east. He is [simultaneously

---

[1] Alternative text: एको भूतश्चरति

[2] Alternative text: *Eko bḥūtaś-carati*

present] with all of them. He alone dwells within [the hearts of] all people, and that is why He is called One (meaning, He alone exists).

Prāṇān – It means lives.

Saṁbhakṣya – having eaten or after eating [them]; *Saṁsṛjati* – creates; *Visṛjati* – He lets go or removes; *Prāṇān* – to all lives; *Sākam* – together.

Dakṣināḥ pratyañca udañcaḥ prāñcaḥ – It means towards the south, west, north, and east.

Eko'bhūdantaś-carati – *Ekaḥ abhūt antaḥ carati*: *Ekaḥ* means one or alone; *abhūt* means was or happened; *antaḥ* means inside; *carati* means moves.

Lord Śiva creates the world (*sṛṣṭi* सृष्टि), sustains it and nourishes it (*sthiti* स्थिति), and then absorbs it (*laya* or *pralaya* लय or प्रलय) within Himself. He again creates it, and thus, the cycle of creation and dissolution goes on. But He ever remains one, one and the same; He never changes. When devotees go to holy places, He is always with them. He lives in their hearts – *Īśvaraḥ sarva-bhūtānāṁ hṛdeśe'rjuna tiṣṭhati* (*Bhagavad Gītā* 18.61) – O *Arjuna*, God resides in the hearts of all living beings.

4.11 अथ कस्मादुच्यते रुद्रः यस्मादृषिभिर्-नान्यैर्-भक्तैर्-द्रुतमस्य रूपमुपलभ्यते तस्मादुच्यते रुद्रः ।

Atha kasmāducyate Rudraḥ yasmā-dṛṣibhir-nānyair-bhaktair-drutamasya rūpa-mupalabhyate tasmā-ducyate Rudraḥ |

> Why is He called Rudra? He is called Rudra because seers can instantly (*drutam*) have His vision (meaning, realize *Brahman*), whereas other [ordinary] devotees cannot.

It is so amazing how the sages have defined the word Rudra in different ways:

Ruṁ drāvayati iti Rudraḥ (रुं द्रावयति इति रुद्रः) – One who dissolves or destroys fear is called Rudra; *ru* (रु) means fear and *dru* (द्रु) means to dissolve or melt.

Rodayati ātma-vimukhāni iti Rudraḥ (रोदयति आत्मविमुखानि इति रुद्रः) – He makes them cry who have turned away from the Self, the Divinity within.

Rodati (रोदति) – He cries [when His devotees suffer].

In the present mantra, the word Rudra is identified with the word *drutam*, meaning instantly.

4.12 [1]**अथ कस्मादुच्यते ईशानः यः सर्वान् देवानीशते ईशानीभिर्-जननीभिश्च शक्तिभिः। अभित्वा शूर नो नुमो दुग्धा**

---

[1] ईशानमस्य जगतः स्वदृशां चक्षुरीश्वरम्।
ईशानमिन्द्रसूरयः सर्वेषामपि सर्वदा॥ Linga II.18.22

इव धेनवः। ईशानमस्य जगतः स्वर्दृशमीशानमिन्द्र तस्थुष इति तस्मादुच्यते ईशानः।

Atha kasmāducyate Īśānaḥ yaḥ sarvān devānīśate īśānībhir-jananībhiśca śaktibhiḥ | Abhitvā śūra no numo dugdhā iva dhenavaḥ | Īśānamsya jagataḥ svardṛśa-mīśāna-mindra tasthuṣa iti tasmāducyate Īśānaḥ |

Why is He called the Ruler (*Īśāna*)? [Because] He, through His powers of ruling and creation, reigns over all the gods (*devas*).

[Gods are praying to Rudra], "O Mighty One, we approach You [for your blessings] the way cows are approached for their milk, and we bow down to You. O *Indra*, You, with a heavenly look, are called *Īśāna* because You are the Lord of [the world, consisting of] movable and immovable [objects].

Īś (ईश्) – to rule; *Īśāna* – ruler or Lord.; *Īśate* – He rules; *Īśānībhiḥ* – His quality or power of ruling; *Jananībhiḥ* – by His quality or power of creation; *Śaktibhiḥ* – by His power; *Śūra* – O Mighty One; *Jagataḥ* – of movables; *Tasthu* –

ईशानः सर्वविद्यानां यत्तदीशान उच्यते। Linga II.18.23

Īśānamasya jagataḥ svadṛśāṁ cakṣurīśvaraṁ |

Īśāna-mindra-sūrayaḥ sarveṣāmapi sarvadā ||

Īśānaḥ sarva-vidyānāṁ yat-tadīśāna ucyate |

immovables; *Svardṛśa* (स्वर्दृश) – one with a heavenly look or appearance.

Lord Śiva, with His qualities of ruling and creation, reigns the world. The gods (*devas*) are praising Him and prostrating before Him because He is the ruler of the movables as well as immovables.

In the mantra, Lord Śiva is addressed as *Indra* – *Indra* is the chief god (*deva* or *devatā*) who rules heaven. It is Lord Śiva, who as *Indra*, rules the heaven.

The *Mahā-Nārāyaṇa Upaniṣad* XXI.1 says:

> ईशानः सर्वविद्यानामीश्वरः सर्वभूतानां । ब्रह्मादिपतिर्-ब्रह्मणोऽधिपतिर्-ब्रह्मा शिवो मे अस्तु सदाशिवोम् ॥
>
> *Īśānaḥ sarva-vidyānā-mīśvaraḥ sarva-bhūtānām | Brahmādipatir-brahmaṇo'-dhipatir-brahmā śivo me astu Sadāśivom ||*
>
> He (Lord Śiva or *Brahman*) is *Īśāna*, the Lord of all knowledge and living beings, the preserver of the Vedas, and the Lord of *Brahmā* (*Hiraṇyagarbha* हिरण्यगर्भ). He may become benevolent towards me; I am eternal Śiva whose symbol is Om.

In this mantra, the devotee is meditating on *Īśāna*, and when he says '*Sadāśivom* (सदाशिवोम्),' he is identifying himself with Śiva or *Brahman*. *Sadāśivom* stands for *Sadāśivo'ham*

(*Sadā-Śivaḥ Aham*) or *Sadāśivo'm* (*Sadā-Śivaḥ Om*) – (सदाशिवोऽहम् – सदाशिव: अहम् or सदाशिवोऽम् – सदाशिव: ओम्). *Sadāśiva* means eternal Śiva or *Brahman.*

4.13 अथ कस्मादुच्यते भगवान् महेश्वरः यस्माद्-भक्तान् ज्ञानेन भजत्यनुगृह्णाति च वाचं संसृजति विसृजति च सर्वान् भावान् परित्यज्यात्मज्ञानेन योगैश्वर्येण महति महीयते तस्मादुच्यते भगवान् महेश्वरः ।

Atha kasmāducyate bhagavān Maheśvaraḥ yasmād-bhaktān jñānena bhajatyanu-gṛhṇāti ca vācaṁ saṁsṛjati visṛjati ca sarvān bhāvān parityajyātma-jñānena yogaiśvaryeṇa mahati mahīyate tasmā-ducyate Bhagavān Maheśvaraḥ |

> Why is He called exalted *Maheśvara*? Being compassionate towards His devotees, He grants them the spiritual knowledge. He creates the speech [so that the devotees can express their love for Him and sing the songs of His glory], and [at the same time] He gets the speech vanished [because no speech or any other sense can reach Him, who is *Brahman*]. By forsaking everything, and with the Self-knowledge and the supremacy of yoga, He rejoices in His own glory, the highest state of existence, and therefore, He is addressed as exalted *Maheśvara*.

Bhajati – He grants; *Ātma-jñānena* – with the knowledge of the Self; *Yogaiśvaryeṇa* – through supremacy of yoga.

Sarvān bhāvān parityajya – It means by forsaking everything.

Mahati mahīyate – Lord Siva enjoys His own glory. This is equivalent to this common phrase, '*Śivaḥ ramayati nija-ramaṇam* (शिवः रमयति निजरमणम्)' – Śiva rejoices in His own ecstasy.

Literally, *Maheśvara* means the Supreme or Great Lord.

4.14 तदेतद्-रुद्रचरितम् ||४||

Tadetad-Rudra-Caritam ||4||

These are the acts of Rudra (Lord Śiva).

Mantra 4 glorifies Rudra by very beautifully explaining His various epithets.

|| Thus, ends Mantra 4 ||

|| ॐ ||

Mantra 5

This mantra explains how to meditate and attain liberation (*mokṣa*).

5.1 [1]एषो ह देवः प्रदिशोऽनु सर्वाः पूर्वो ह जातः स उ गर्भे अन्तः । स एव जातः स जनिष्यमाणः प्रत्यङ्जनास्तिष्ठति सर्वतोमुखः ।

Eṣo ha devaḥ pradiśo'nu sarvaḥ pūrvo ha jātaḥ sa u garbhe antaḥ | *Sa eva jātaḥ sa janiṣyamāṇaḥ pratyaṅ-janās-tiṣṭhati sarvato-mukhaḥ* |

> This Deity (Rudra) is present in all quarters. He indeed is the first-born and is inside [every] womb. He alone was born, and He is the one who will take birth [again]. He, who is omnipresent, resides in [the hearts of] all people [as their *Ātman*, the Inner Self].

---

[1] एषो हि देवः प्रदिशोऽनुसर्वाः पूर्वो हि जातः स उ गर्भे अन्तः ।
स एव जातः स जनिष्यमाणः प्रत्यङ्मुखास्तिष्ठति सर्वतोमुखः ॥ Liṅga II.18.26
Eṣo hi devaḥ pradiśo'nu-sarvāḥ pūrvo hi jātaḥ sa u garbhe antaḥ |
Sa eva jātaḥ sa janiṣyamāṇaḥ pratyaṅ-mukhās-tiṣṭhati sarvato-mukhaḥ ||

Pūrvo ha jātaḥ – It means, 'one who was indeed born in the beginning, i.e., before the creation' or 'one who is first-born.' This is to show that there was no one before Rudra. Rudra as *Brahman* – the Absolute Truth – is always present; He does not take birth. It only means that He was there before the manifestation of this world.

Sa u garbhe antaḥ – *Sa u* means, 'He indeed,' *Garbhe* means, 'in the womb,' and *antaḥ* means 'within or in the interior.' Thus, Rudra is inside every womb as the consciousness of the fetus. The word *garbhe* also means 'in the middle,' and *anta* means, 'the end.' Rudra is in the middle manifested as this universe, and He alone will remain after the dissolution of the present world.

In the *Bhagavad Gītā* XIV.3, Lord *Kṛṣṇa* says:

मम योनिर्महद्-ब्रह्म तस्मिन् गर्भं दधाम्यहम् ।
सम्भवः सर्वभूतानां ततो भवति भारत ॥

Mama yonir–mahad-Brahma
tasmin garbhaṁ dadhāmyaham |
Sambhavaḥ sarva - bhūtānaṁ
tato bhavati Bhārata ||

O Arjuna, *Prakṛti* (प्रकृति – primordial nature), which is known as great-*Brahma*, is the womb [of all living beings]. In that womb, I place the seed of life, and from that union, all are born.

The primordial nature is the material cause of the universe. It is material energy, whereas, Lord Rudra or Lord Śiva is the

Consciousness, the life force. (Note: *Śrī Kṛṣṇa* and Lord Śiva are the names of the same Ultimate Truth). All living beings are born due to the union of the material energy and the Consciousness. In fact, the primordial nature too is a manifestation of Śiva, and thus, all living beings come-forth from Śiva.

Sa eva jātaḥ sa janiṣyamāṇaḥ – It means, 'He alone is born, and He will be born [again].' It is Rudra who has manifested as this present world and will manifest again. The cycle of creation (*sṛṣṭi* सृष्टि), sustenance (*sthiti* स्थिति), dissolution (*pralaya* प्रलय), and creation one more time goes on.

Pratyaṅ tiṣṭhati (प्रत्यङ् तिष्ठति) – It means 'dwells within.' *Pratyaṅ* is singular, nominative case of *pratyañc* (प्रत्यञ्च्); one of the meanings of *pratyañc* is 'inward or individual soul.'

Sarvato-mukhaḥ – It means, 'one who has faces in all directions,' i.e., He is omnipresent.

Śvetāśvatara Upaniṣad, Mantra II.16 is verbatim of the above mantra:

> *Eṣo ha devaḥ pradiśo'nu sarvāḥ*
> *pūrvo ha jataḥ sa u garbhe antaḥ* |
> *Sa eva jātaḥ sa janiṣyamāṇaḥ*
> *pratyaṅ-janās-tiṣṭhati sarvato-mukhaḥ* ||

5.2 एको रुद्रो न द्वितीयाय तस्मै य इमाँल्लोकानीशत ईशानीभिः । प्रत्यङ्जनास्तिष्ठति सञ्चुकोचान्तकाले संसृज्य विश्वाभुवनानि गोप्ता ।

Eko Rudro na dvitīyāya tasmai ya imānl-lokānīśata īśānībhiḥ | Pratyaṅ-janās-tiṣṭhati sañcukocānta-kāle saṁsṛjya viśvā-bhuvanāni goptā |

> Rudra is the only one; there is no one else as a second. He reigns over all these worlds with His powers. He dwells in [the hearts of] all living beings [as their Inner Self]. After creating all the worlds, in the end [at the time of dissolution], He, their Protector, withdraws them into Himself.

Eko Rudro (*Rudraḥ*) – It means only Rudra exists, there is no one besides Him as a second. It is Rudra who manifests Himself as these *Lokas* or worlds – *Bhu*, *Bhuva*, *Sva*, *Maha*, *Jana*, *Tapa*, and *Satya* (for the explanation of these worlds, see the commentary on Mantra 2.14). After manifesting as these worlds, or in other words, after creating these worlds, He, with His powers, reigns over them.

Sañcukocānta-kāle – Sañcukoca anta-kāle: *sañcukoca* – He withdraws into Himself; *Anta-kāle* – in the end [at the time of dissolution].

Saṁsṛjya viśvā-bhuvanāni goptā – After creating the worlds, He becomes their protector and maintains them.

Śvetāśvatara Upaniṣad, Mantra III.2 has the similar words:

> *Eko hi Rudro na dvitīyāya tasthur*
> *ya imānl-lokānīśata īśānībhiḥ* |
> *Pratyaṅ janās-tiṣṭhati sañcukocānta-kāle*

saṁsṛjya viśvā bhuvanāni gopāḥ ||

5.3 [1]**यो योनिं योनिमधितिष्ठत्येको येनेदं सर्वं विचरति सर्वम् | तमीशानं वरदं देवमीड्यं निचाय्येमां शान्तिमत्यन्तमेति |**

Yo yonim̐ yonimadhi-tiṣṭhatyeko yenedaṁ sarvaṁ vicarati sarvam | Tamīśānaṁ varadaṁ deva-mīḍyaṁ nicāyyemāṁ śānti-matyanta-meti |

> He alone presides over every living being, and everything moves because of Him. By worshipping this adorable, self-effulgent Lord, who grants boons, [the seeker attains] the boundless Supreme Peace.

Yoni – The word *yoni* has two meanings; one is the womb, and the other is species. It is Rudra who is in the organ of birth and manifests as all species, i.e., all living beings.

Nicāyya – nicāy means to worship, honor, perceive; *nicāyya* means by worshipping or honoring; *Adhitiṣṭhati* – He governs or presides over.

Śvetaśvatara Upaniṣad, Mantra IV.11 has the similar words:

> *Yo yonim̐ yonimadhi-tiṣṭhatyeko*
> *Yasmin-nidaṁ saṁ ca vi caiti sarvam* |
> *Tamīśānaṁ varadaṁ deva-mīḍyaṁ*

---

[1] अधितिष्ठति योनिं यो योनिं वाचैक ईशवर: | Liṅga II.18.39
Adhitiṣṭhati yonim̐ yo yonim̐ vācaika Īśvaraḥ |

nicāyyemāṁ śānti-matyanta-meti ||

5.4 [1]क्षमां हित्वा हेतुजालस्य मूलं बुद्धया सञ्चितं स्थापयित्वा तु रुद्रे । रुद्रमेकत्वमाहुः शाश्वतं वै पुराणमिषमूर्जेण पशवोऽनुनामयन्तं मृत्युपाशान् ।

Kṣamāṁ hitvā hetujālasya mūlaṁ buddhyā sañcitaṁ sthāpayitvā tu Rudre | Rudra-mekatva-māhuḥ śāśvataṁ vai purāṇa-miṣamūrjeṇa paśavo'nu-nāmayantaṁ mṛtyu-pāśān |

> By abandoning [ignorance like] forgiveness, [etc.,] which is the basis of all bondage, and by mentally surrendering all accumulated [deeds, good as well as bad] to Lord Rudra, [the aspirant] becomes one with Lord Rudra – who is said to be eternal, ancient, nourishing, and worthy of worship. [Compassionate Lord Rudra], through His vigor, [protects] all living beings from the fear of death.

Kṣamāṁ hitvā hetu-jālasya mūlaṁ – *Kṣamāṁ hitvā* means 'by abandoning forgiveness.' *Hetu-jālasya mūlaṁ* means 'the cause of the basis of bondage'; *jāla* means 'net' or 'one which binds.'

---

[1]तृष्णां छित्त्वा हेतुजालस्य मूलं बुद्धया चिन्त्यं स्थापयित्वा च रुद्रे ॥ Liṅga II.18.40
Tṛṣṇāṁ chittvā hetujālasya mūlaṁ buddhyā cintyaṁ sthāpayitvā ca Rudre ||

Here, strangely, the forgiveness (*kṣamā*) is considered as the cause of bondage, which must be given up. Usually, *Kṣamā* or forgiveness is part of Dharma (see the commentary on Mantra 1.3i), which must not be abandoned; *kṣamā* is considered as a great virtue. Yes, it is a great virtue, but for a spiritual person, the thought of forgiving someone is a hindrance to his spiritual quest. As explained later in Mantra 5.12, when the aspirant thinks that he has forgiven someone, it is not his greatness; instead, it is his ignorance, his ego. Any of his sufferings are the result of his own past malicious deeds; the other person is only a medium, not the cause of his sufferings. To whom is the aspirant forgiving, and for what? It is not the other person's fault, though it appears that way.

Buddhyā sañcitaṁ sthāpayitvā tu Rudre – It means mentally establishing all his accumulated karmas in Rudra. One must mentally surrender all his actions, good as well as bad, to Lord Śiva. This is the highest state of devotion.

Ekatvam – oneness. The aspirant becomes one with Rudra, meaning, the seeker realizes the oneness of the *Atman* and *Brahman.*

Iṣa (इष) – *Iṣa* means juicy, fertile, possessing sap and strength, well-fed – it is nourishment. Lord Rudra provides nourishment through food and thus takes care of all. It should be noted that *Iṣa* (इष) is different from *Īśa* (ईश), which means the ruler.

Ūrjeṇa – by vigor, potency, or energy.

Anunā-mayantam – *anunāmayati* is made of two words *anu* + *nāmayati*; it means 'causes to bow or lean towards.' Thus, *anunāmayanta* means one who makes others bow down; People bow down to the one who is worthy of worship, therefore, I have translated '*Anunā-mayantam*' as 'Worthy of worship'.

Paśavo (*Paśavaḥ*) – It refers to the worldly people who are bonded due to their own past actions. Literally, *paśavaḥ* means animals. With Lord Śiva's grace, aspirant's all bondages are destroyed and he becomes one with Śiva.

Mṛtyu-pāśān – *Mṛtyu* means death, and *pāśa* means rope or shackle. Everyone is bonded by the chains of birth and death.

5.5 तदेतेनात्मन्नेतेनार्धचतुर्थेन मात्रेण शान्तिं संसृजति पशु-पाशविमोक्षणम् ।

Tade-tenātman-netenārdha-caturthena mātreṇa śāntiṁ saṁsṛjati paśupāśa-vimokṣaṇam |

> He (Lord Rudra), by granting the Self-Knowledge (the spiritual knowledge) through the fourth *mātrā*, which is called the half *mātrā*, destroys all bondage and bestows the supreme peace.

Tade-tenātman-netenārdha-caturthena mātreṇa may be broken as *Tat etena ātman etena ardha-caturthena mātreṇa.*

Tad (*Tat*) – It means He, meaning Rudra.

Etena Ātman – *Etena* means by this, and *Ātman* stands for the *Ātma-Jñāna* or the knowledge of the Self or the spiritual knowledge. Thus, *etena Ātman* means 'with the help of Self-Knowledge.'

Ardha-caturthena mātreṇa – *Ardha* means half, *caturthen mātreṇa* means by the fourth *mātrā*; the fourth *mātrā* is the *ardha-matrā*, meaning the half *mātrā*. To understand what the *mātrās* are, one needs to know the significance of OM, which is explained later.

Paśupāśa-vimokṣaṇaṁ – Literally, *paśu* (पशु) means an animal, pāśa (पाश) means the rope which binds animals and *vimokṣaṇa* (विमोक्षण) means liberation. All living beings (*jīvas* जीव) and even the gods (*devas*) are considered as *paśus* (animals). Lord Śiva is their master – *Paśupati* (पशुपति). Rudra frees gods as well as living beings of all their bondages (meaning ignorance).

All living beings are tied with the shackles of their own accumulated actions (karmas), good and bad. Based on their actions, they go through the cycles of births and deaths. When a person does good deeds, he goes to heaven; when he performs immensely good deeds, he becomes a *devatā (*god*)*. Either way, after enjoying the results of his good deeds in heaven, he goes back to the world to be a human. Of course, bad deeds lead to miseries in the next lives. Thus, the cycle of transmigration goes on without an end until the *Jīva*'s (individual soul's) ignorance (*Avidyā* अविद्या) is destroyed by the spiritual knowledge (*Jñāna* ज्ञान). One way to obtain the spiritual knowledge, the knowledge of the Self (*Ātma-Jñāna* आत्मज्ञान), is to be a staunch devotee of Lord Śiva. The aspirant must detach himself from the worldly pleasures, give up all his desires, and mentally surrender all his actions to Lord Śiva. With spiritual practice (*sādhanā* साधना) and by Śiva's grace (*anugraha* अनुग्रह), his ignorance gets destroyed, and he realizes that he is not different from Śiva; he experiences the oneness of the *Ātman* and *Brahman*. He is free from the worldly bondage.

Lord Śiva is called *Paśupati*, the Lord of all *Jīvas* (individual souls) and *devas* (gods); all are bound by the shackles of ignorance, and they could be freed only by the grace of Lord Śiva.

To understand what the *mātrās* are and what their significance is, one must first know what OM is.

Significance of OM

Praṇava (प्रणव) is also called OM (ओम्), and its symbol is ॐ. It is the most sacred word or sound in the *Sanātana* Dharma (Hindu Dharma).

Kaṭha Upaniṣad (कठ उपनिषद्) II.16 proclaims, '*etad hi eva akṣaraṁ Brahma* (एतद् हि एव अक्षरं ब्रह्म)' – this syllable [OM] is indeed *Brahman*; here *Akṣaraṁ* means syllable, which is OM. *Akṣaraṁ* also means indestructible; thus, this phrase could also be translated as 'this indestructible [OM] is verily *Brahman.*'

Mahā-Nārāyaṇa Upaniṣad (महानारायण उपनिषद्) 33.1 says the same thing: *Om iti eka akṣaraṁ Brahma* (ओम् इति एक अक्षरं ब्रह्म) – the one-syllable OM is *Brahman*, the Ultimate Truth. As it was said before, *Akṣara* means syllable OM, *eka* means one; thus, *eka akṣaraṁ* means One-syllable OM. Per Sanskrit poetry rules too, the word OM is one syllable. The OM, when pronounced as one syllable – instead of breaking it into three of its constituting sounds *A*, *U*, and *M*, as explained below – is the name of *Brahman.*

Since Rudra is another name of *Brahman*, OM represents Rudra.

Three *Mātrās* (मात्रा)

As explained in the commentary on Mantra 3.5, the word OM is made up of three letters – *A* (अ), *U* (उ), and *M* (म्). Per Sanskrit grammar, when vowel *U* follows vowel *A*, both together change to *O*: अ + उ = ओ, or *A* + *U* = *O*, and that is why *A*+*U*+*M* is written and pronounced as OM [as in ***home*** or ***dome***]. *A*, *U*, and *M* are the three *mātrās* that form the one-syllable word OM. One may alternatively write the word OM as AUM to show all the three *mātrās* in English; however, one should keep it in mind that it must be pronounced as OM, as in ***home*** or ***dome***.

I will explain below how the three constituents of OM are to be pronounced, or the reader may refer to Appendix B.

- *A* is to be pronounced like the sound ***a*** in ***a***bove [not as Alphabet letter 'A'],
- *U* as the sound ***u*** in p***u***t [not as Alphabet letter 'U'], and,
- *M* as the sound ***m*** in si***m***ple [not as Alphabet letter 'M']; it is a humming sound 'mmm.'

<u>*Māṇḍūkya Upaniṣad* (माण्डूक्य उपनिषद्)</u>

The best description of OM is given in the *Māṇḍūkya Upaniṣad*, which consists of only 12 mantras. Mantra 1 says: All this [world] is syllable OM (Om *iti etad akṣaraṁ idaṁ sarvam* – ओम् इति एतद् अक्षरं इदं सर्वम्). Thus, OM is not only *Brahman*, but this world, too, is not different from OM, meaning this world is *Brahman's* manifestation. Mantra 2 confirms the same idea: All this [world] is indeed *Brahman* (*Sarvaṁ hi etad Brahma* – सर्वं हि एतद् ब्रह्म). Here, I have translated the word *akṣara* as syllable, but it also means imperishable. Thus, we may say, OM indeed is eternal and ever-existing.

Mantra 2 also says: 'This *Ātman*, the Self within all living beings, is *Brahman* (*Ayaṁ Ātmā Brahma* – अयं आत्मा ब्रह्म). – This shows the oneness of the *Ātman* and *Brahman*; this is the non-dual philosophy, *Advaita-vāda* (अद्वैतवाद), according to which the Inner Self of all living beings is not different from *Brahman* – the Ultimate Reality, the Ultimate Truth, or God Absolute.

Mantra 2 further describes the Self having four phases or aspects: स: अयम् आत्मा चतुष्पात् – *Saḥ ayaṁ Ātmā catuṣpāt* – The Self has four quarters or aspects. The word *Catuṣ* or *Catuḥ* (चतु:) means four and *Pāt* (पात्) or *Pād* (पाद्) means foot or quarter. However, in this context, *Ātman* does not have any parts or quarters, but He manifests in different phases, or He has four aspects.

There are three states through which the Self goes through – waking, dream, and deep sleep. According to the *Māṇḍūkya Upaniṣad*, the first *mātrā A* (अ) of AUM (OM) stands for the Self when he is in the waking state. In this state, he is known as *Vaiśvānara* (वैश्वानर). *Vaiśvānara* is the first aspect of the Self. In this state, the Consciousness is outward-turned (Mantras 3 & 9).

The second *mātrā U* (उ) stands for the Self when he is in the dream state; in this state, he is known as *Taijasa* (तैजस). *Taijasa* is the second aspect of the Self. In this state, the Consciousness is inward-turned (Mantras 4 &10).

The third *mātrā M* (म्) stands for the Self when he is in the deep sleep state; in this state, he is known as *Prājña* (प्राज्ञ). *Prājña* is the third aspect of the Self. In the state of deep sleep, one neither desires nor dreams, and one remains blissful (Mantras 5 &11).

Mantra 8 says, 'This *Ātman* is identified with OM when OM is a single syllable [without being broken into its three constituent *mātrās A*, *U*, and *M*].'

According to Mantra 12, the last mantra of the *Māṇḍūkya Upaniṣad*, OM, as one syllable or in its part-less aspect, is called the Fourth (*Caturtha* - चतुर्थ). In this state, the Consciousness is neither outward-turned nor inward-turned; one is very quiet, peaceful, and blissful. The fourth is the *Ātman*, the Self, which must be realized. The fourth aspect is transcendental (*Avyavahārya* - अव्यवहार्य), having no phenomenal existence (*Prapañcopaśama* - प्रपञ्चोपशम), Supreme Bliss (Śiva - शिव), and non-dual (*Advaita* - अद्वैत). Thus, the Syllable OM is indeed the Self or *Ātman*.

Scriptures also call the fourth aspect as *Turīya* (तुरीय), meaning the fourth. The fourth aspect, which is called OM, is also present in the three states of waking, dreaming, and sleeping. The word *Turīya* is masculine gender when it refers to the *Ātman*, the Self. Referring to the fourth state, it is used as a feminine gender *Turīyā* (तुरीया).

At microcosmic (*Vyaṣṭi* - व्यष्टि) level, the Supreme Consciousness is called *Ātman*, the individual Self, whereas at macrocosmic (*Samaṣṭi* - समष्टि) level it is known as *Brahman*, the Ultimate Truth. Related names for both cases are given in the following Table:

TABLE V.1

State (Aspect)	**Microcosm** (Individual) ***Ātman***	**Macrocosm** (Universal) ***Brahman***
Waking	*Vaiśvānara*; '*A*'	*Virāṭ*
Dream	*Taijasa*; '*U*'	*Hiraṇyagarbha*
Deep sleep	*Prājña*; '*M*'	*Īśvara*
Fourth (*Turīyā*)	'OM'– pervades all states and forms; Oneness of *Ātman-Brahman*	

Here, OM as one syllable is the fourth or the half *mātrā* (*ardha-mātrā*).

The explanation of OM given above will help in understanding the following Mantras 5.6 through 5.9.

5.6 या सा प्रथमा मात्रा ब्रह्मदेवत्या रक्ता वर्णेन यस्तां ध्यायते नित्यं स गच्छेद्-ब्रह्मपदम् ।

Yā sā prathamā mātrā Brahma-devatyā raktā varṇena yastāṁ dhyāyate nityaṁ sa gacched-Brahma-padam |

> The first *mātrā* [*A* - अ)], which is of the red color, is associated with *Brahmā*. One who continuously meditates on the red colored first *mātrā* attains the abode of *Brahmā*.

After discussing the *ardha-mātrā*, now the mantra is explaining what happens when the seeker meditates on the first *mātrā A*. In the triad of Gods, Lord *Brahmā* is the creator.

5.7 या सा द्वितीया मात्रा विष्णुदेवत्या कृष्णवर्णेन यस्तां ध्यायते नित्यं स गच्छेद्-वैष्णवं पदम् ।

Yā sā dvitīyā mātrā Viṣṇu-devatyā kṛṣṇa-varṇena yastāṁ dhyāyate nityaṁ sa gacched-Vaiṣṇavaṁ padam |

> The second *mātrā* [*U* - उ], which is of the black color, is associated with Lord *Viṣṇu*. Onc who continuously meditates on the black colored second *mātrā* attains the abode of Lord *Viṣṇu*.

The mantra is explaining what happens when the seeker meditates on the second *mātrā U*. Lord *Viṣṇu* is the preserver or protector of the world.

5.8 या सा तृतीया मात्रा ईशानदेवत्या कपिला वर्णेन यस्तां ध्यायते नित्यं स गच्छेदैशानं पदम् ।

Yā sā tṛiīyā mātrā Īśāna-devatyā kapilā varṇena yastāṁ dhyāyate nityaṁ sa gacche-daiśānaṁ padam |

> The third *mātrā* [*M* - म्], which is of the tawny color, is associated with Lord *Īśāna*. One who

> continuously meditates on the tawny-colored third *mātrā* attains the abode of Lord *Ĩśāna.*

Now, the mantra is explaining what happens when the seeker meditates on the third *mātrā M.* Lord *Ĩśāna* is the one who reigns over the world or who brings order to the world.

In Sanskrit, the world is called *saṁsāra* (संसार). *Saṁsarati iti saṁsāraḥ* (संसरति इति संसार:) – one which flows, meaning undergoes transmigration, is called *saṁsāra.* Nothing stays at the same place. What you see today may not be there tomorrow. Tomorrow, something else will come forth. The seed, when sowed and adequately nourished, becomes a tree. The tree gives fruits having seeds. The seeds of the fruit become new trees. This is *saṁsāra.* A baby is born; the baby grows and becomes an adult who procreates, and thus, a new baby is born – this is *saṁsāsra.* A *Jīva* is conceived and then born, he grows, experiences joys and sorrows, becomes old, dies, and once again conceived and born – this is *saṁsāra.* A world is created (*sṛṣṭi* सृष्टि), stays for some time (*sthiti* स्थिति), then the end of the world comes (*pralaya* प्रलय – dissolution), and once again a new world is created – this is *saṁsāra.* The cycle goes on. It is *Ĩśāna* who brings this kind of order to the world.

We saw in Mantras 5.6, 5.7, and 5.8 that the three *mātrās A, U,* and *M* are associated with *Brahmā*, *Viṣṇu*, and *Ĩśāna*, respectively. Some scriptures may describe them differently, especially the third *mātrā M*; despite that, every scripture describes OM as another name for *Brahman.*

Now, let us see what Mantras 37 to 39 of *Śrīmad Bhāgavatam* XII.6 say about OM:

> When Lord *Brahmā*, the Creator, who occupies the highest position, was in deep meditation, a transcendental and subtle sound [which is called *Anāhata Nāda* अनाहत नाद] arose from the cavity of his heart. Such a sound could be clearly perceived only when the mind is completely silent and tranquil. By concentrating on such sound, yogīs cleanse their hearts of all impurities and attain *Mokṣha* (मोक्ष), i.e., liberation. From that transcendental sound exhibited the sacred syllable OM, also known as *Oṅkara* (ओङ्कार), consisting of three *mātrās* [*A*, *U*, and *M*]. OM, having an unmanifest origin, manifests itself and shines [in the hearts of aspirants]. OM is the representation of *Brahman* – the Ultimate Reality, or *Paramātman* – the Supreme Self or God.

Śrīmad Bhāgavatam XII.6, Mantra 42 further says:

> From the syllable OM unveiled three sounds of the Alphabet *A* (अ), *U* (उ), and *M* (म्), which respectively represent:
>
> - Three *guṇas* (गुण) or three modes of nature [*Sattva*, *Rajas*, and *Tamas*].
>
>   Thus, (i) *Mātrā A* represents *Sattva* सत्त्व – goodness, purity, (ii) *Mātrā U* represents *Rajas* रजस् – passion, activity, and (iii) *Mātrā M*

represents *Tamas* तमस् – ignorance, darkness, lethargy.

- Three names or Vedas [*Ṛgveda*, *Yajurveda*, and *Sāmaveda*].

  Thus, (i) *Mātrā A* represents *Ṛgveda* ऋग्वेद, (ii) *Mātrā U* represents *Yajurveda* यजुर्वेद, and (iii) *Mātrā M* represents *Sāmaveda* सामवेद.

- Three objects, i.e., worlds or *Lokas* लोक [*Bhuḥ*, *Bhuvaḥ*, and *Svaḥ*].

  Thus, (i) *Mātrā A* represents *Bhuḥ* भूः – earth, (ii) *Mātrā U* represents *Bhuvaḥ* भुवः – mid-region, and (iii) *Mātrā M* represents *Svaḥ* स्वः – heaven.

- Three states of existence [waking, dream, and deep sleep].

  Thus, (i) *Mātrā A* represents the waking state – *Jāgrat* जाग्रत्, (ii) *Mātrā U* represents the dream state – *Svapna* स्वप्न, and (iii) *Mātrā M* represents the state of deep sleep – *Suṣupti* सुषुप्ति.

The reader must note that OM is another name of *Brahman*, the Ultimate Truth; it is ever-existing in its unmanifest state. Just before the time of the actual creation, it manifested as *Anāhata Nāda*, the transcendental, subtle sound, in the heart of *Brahmā* when he was in deep meditation. This sound is also known as *Śabda-Brahma*. The words *Nāda* and *Śabda* mean the sound; this was a cosmic sound.

Similarly, yogīs hear the same sound when they are in deep meditation. You don't need ears to hear this sound, even a deaf person can hear it. The *Anāhata Nāda* could be heard as the sound 'OooMmmm,' or hymning sound 'mmm,' or as a sound of a conch, flute, or Veena (वीणा *vīṇā* – it is a musical instrument like a Sitar). This sound that yogīs hear is called *ardha-mātrā* (अर्धमात्रा) or the half-*mātrā*. Since this sound is heard during the fourth state of the existence – *Turīyā* (तुरीया) State – it is also called the fourth *mātrā*.

According to the *Śiva-Mahā-Purāṇa*, *Vidyeśvara-Saṁhitā* (शिवमहापुराण, विद्येश्वर-संहिता), Chapter 10:

> Lord Śiva performs five cosmic activities – (i) Creation (*sṛṣṭi* - सृष्टि), (ii) Sustenance (*sthiti* - स्थिति), (iii) Destruction (*saṁhāra* - संहार), (iv) Concealing (*tirobhāva* or *tirodhāna* - तिरोभाव or तिरोधान), and (v) Grace (*anugraha* - अनुग्रह). He respectively performs these five activities as (i) Lord *Brahmā*, (ii) Lord *Viṣṇu*, (iii) Lord Rudra (a manifestation of Śiva; also called *Hara*), (iv) Lord *Maheśa* (a manifestation of Śiva), and (v) Śiva or *Sadā-Śiva* (Śiva Himself).

It is Lord Śiva's Māyā, His deluding power, which prevents His devotees from having His vision. He veils Himself from His devotees until their devotion matures, and they are worthy of having His vision. Having a vision of Śiva means the realization of *Brahman* or experiencing *Brahamn*. The veiling process is called *tirobhāva* or *tirodhāna*. When the devotee develops extreme love for Lord Śiva, with Lord Śiva's grace (*anugraha*), the devotee's heart gets purified, his ignorance gets destroyed, and then Lord Śiva unveils Himself to the devotee.

The *Śiva-Mahā-Purāṇa*, *Kailāsa-Saṁhitā* (शिवमहापुराण, कैलास-संहिता), Chapter 3: This chapter gives an unambiguous description of OM, its three *mātrās*, *ardha-matrā*, and their significance related to the five cosmic activities of Lord Śiva.

> There is no difference between Lord Śiva and *Praṇava* (प्रणव), i.e., OM. It is called *Praṇava* because it is the *Prāṇa* (प्राण) – life-force – of all living beings, from *Brahmā* down to all living beings. OM is constituted of three *mātrās* अ (*A*), उ (*U*), म् (*M*), and its symbol ॐ has a बिन्दु (*Bindu* – dot) and a नाद (*Nāda* – crescent moon) on the top. The *Ardha-mātrā* (अर्द्धमात्रा) or the half *mātrā*, which transcends the three *mātrās*, is in the form of *Nāda* and *Bindu* (crescent and dot). The half *mātrā* cannot be described; it can only be known by the wise.
>
> *Mātrā A* is (i) the great seed, (ii) *Rajas*, and (iii) *Brahmā* – the creator.

Note: रजस् - *Rajas* is the mode of nature having the quality of passion and activity; it is the quality of creativity.

Mātrā U is (i) the womb of *Prakṛti* (प्रकृति), (ii) *Sattva*, and (iii) *Viṣṇu* – the preserver or protector, who sustains the world.

Note: सत्त्व - Sattva is the mode of nature having the quality of goodness and purity.

Mātrā M is (i) *Puruṣa* (पुरुष), the possessor of the great seed, (ii) *Tamas*, and (iii) *Hara* – the destroyer (हर - *Hara* is a name of Śiva).

Note: Being *Puruṣa*, who possesses the seed of creation, it is Lord Śiva who creates and maintains the world through *Brahmā* [the great seed] and *Viṣṇu* [the womb of *Prakṛti*]. तमस् - *Tamas* is the mode of nature having the qualities of ignorance, darkness, and lethargy; this is the quality of destruction.

Bindu (dot) is *Maheśvara* – the one who conceals, meaning the one who prevents devotees from seeing Lord Śiva – *tirobhāva*.

Nāda (crescent moon) is *Sadāśiva* – eternal Śiva, who showers grace on His devotees (*anugraha*).

Nāda is a transcendental, subtle, vibrating sound, which is not different from *Brahman*. This sound must be meditated upon as the half *mātrā* coming from the top of the head (*Sahasrāra Cakra* सहस्रार चक्र).

The reader must bear in mind that *Īśana*, Rudra, *Maheśa*, *Maheśvara*, *Hara*, *Sadāśiva*, etc., are the various names of Lord Śiva, and they may get interchanged for Lord Śiva's five cosmic activities in other scriptures.

[1]The spiritual seeker (*sādhaka*) during his meditation or *japa* (repetition of a mantra) chants the word OM, usually mentally, as *OooMmm* (prolonging *O* and *M*). During his meditation, his eyes must be closed and focused on the space between the two eyebrows (*Ājñā Cakra* – see the commentary on Mantra 2.14). While inhaling, he should chant OM; at the same time, he should listen to the sound OM, which is mentally uttered by him. Then, he should hold his breath, keeping his mind completely quiet, no thought at all. Afterwards, he should breathe out chanting OM while listening to his own voice (OM). He should breathe in again and repeat the process. The period of the silence between the two OMs is the fourth *mātrā* or the *Ardha* (half) *mātrā*. When he is chanting OM, either mentally or loudly, he is, in fact, chanting the three constituting *mātrās* of OM – *A*, *U*, and *M*. The silent period represents one syllable, part-less OM, without breaking it, as explained in the commentary on Mantra 5.5 under the subtitle *Māṇḍūkya Upaniṣad*.

---

[1] A sincere seeker must approach his spiritual guru to learn how to meditate. The method given here is only a hint, not an actual procedure for meditating. There are various mantras and methods for meditating; OM is one of the mantras.

Now, let us see the significance of the fourth *mātrā*.

5.9 या सार्धचतुर्थी मात्रा सर्वदेवत्याऽव्यक्तीभूता खं विचरति शुद्धा स्फटिकसन्निभा वर्णेन यस्तां ध्यायते नित्यं स गच्छेत् पदमनामयम् |

Yā sārdha-caturthī mātrā sarva-devatyā'-vyaktībhūtā khaṁ vicarati śuddhā sphaṭika-sannibhā varṇena yastāṁ dhyāyate nityaṁ sa gacchet padama-nāmayam |

> The fourth *mātrā*, which is called the *ardha* (half) *mātrā*, is beyond the perception of even *devas* (gods); it pervades the space; it is pure; its color resembles a quartz crystal. One who continuously meditates upon it attains liberation (*mokṣa*).

Khaṁ vicarati – *Khaṁ* means 'in space' and *vicarati* means 'roams or pervades;' thus, the meaning of *khaṁ vicarati* is 'it pervades the space.' Thus, the half-*mātrā* is 'all-pervading' since space is an all-pervading part of the universe.

I have already explained what is meant by the *ardha mātrā*. It is not a syllable; it is only a vibrating sound. Per Hindu scriptures, any sound is related to the *Ākāśa Tattva* (आकाश तत्त्व), the Space element. The physical world is made up of five elements or *tattvas* – Space (*Ākāśa* आकाश), Air or Wind (*Vāyu* वायु), Fire (*Agni* अग्नि), Water (*Jala* जल), and Earth

(*Pṛthivī* पृथिवी). Hearing, touch, sight, taste, and smell, respectively, are the functions of the five sense organs – ears, skin, eyes, tongue, and nose. They are respectively associated with the five elements Space, Air, Fire, Water, and Earth. Since the sound is related to the Space element, the mantra says that the *ardha mātrā*, which is a sound, roams (*vicarati*) in the space or pervades the space.

Avyaktibhūtā – It means one which is not visible. Vision or sight is associated with the Fire element. Vision is only one of the five senses. In fact, the *ardha māṭrā* cannot be perceived by any of the senses. That is why I have interpreted it as beyond any perception. The reader must note that no ears are needed to hear the *Anāhata* sound that is experienced by the yogīs.

Sarva-devatyāḥ – It means by all *Devas* or gods. The *ardha mātrā* is such a hidden secret that it cannot be comprehended by anyone, including the celestial beings (gods).

Sphaṭika-sannibhā varṇena – It means 'like the color of a quartz crystal.' Pure quartz has no color.

Padamanāmayam – The word is made up of *padam* + *anāmayam*. *Pada* means a post, position, or abode, and *anāmaya* means free from disease. One attains the abode, which is beyond any disease or misery. Therefore, *Padamanāmaya* is usually translated as liberation. Also, *Anāmaya* is one of the names of Lord Śiva, and therefore, *Padamanāmaya* means the abode of Lord Śiva. Reaching the abode of Lord Śiva is equivalent to attaining *mokṣa* or liberation. Śiva means bliss, and thus, *Padamanāmaya* also means the abode of Bliss.

The aspirant worships Lord Śiva in the form of a *Liṅga*, which is placed on a *Yoni*. *Liṅga* means a mark or symbol – it is a symbol of Lord Śiva. *Yoni* means seat or place of rest; *liṅga* is of cylindrical shape with a curved top. The *liṅga* could be made of clay, stone, or metal. But the naturally formed quartz crystal is the most auspicious *liṅga*.

5.10 तदेतदुपासीत मुनयो वाग्वदन्ति न तस्य ग्रहणमयं पन्था विहित उत्तरेण येन देवा यान्ति येन पितरो येन ऋषयः परमपरं परायणं चेति ।

Tade-tadupāsīta munayo vāg-vadanti na tasya grahaṇa-mayaṁ panthā vihita uttareṇa yena devā yānti yena pitaro yena ṛṣayaḥ parama-paraṁ parāyaṇaṁ ceti |

> Holy men say he (the aspirant) must worship this (the fourth *mātrā*). [One who worships it] becomes free from the bondage of all his karmas. This is the ordained northern path that gods (*devas*), manes, and sages take; it is a distant supreme path, which is their last refuge.

Tadetadupāsīta – The word may be broken as *tad-etad-upāsīta*. *Tad* means that, meaning he – the aspirant. *Etad* means this; it relates to the fourth *mātrā*. *Upāsīta* means one should worship. The whole phrase means that the aspirant must worship or meditate on the fourth *mātrā*.

Na tasya grahaṇa-mayaṁ – *Grahaṇa* means seizing, holding, or grabbing of something. *Grahaṇa-mayam* refers to the accumulated karmas whose fruits are yet to be experienced. All the karmas or deeds of the aspirant, who meditates on the fourth *mātrā*, are destroyed. Karmas are the cause of bondage; since there are no more karmas in his account, he is free of any bondage.

Para, *apara*, and *parāyaṇa* – *Para* means supreme, *apara* means distant, and *parāyaṇa* means refuge. This northern path is a distant, supreme path, which is the final refuge or the ultimate resort.

Based on his virtuous karmas, the departed soul travels by one of these two paths – northerly and southerly. The former is effulgent, whereas the latter is dark. I will underscore: these two paths are for those people who have performed righteous actions.

[1]Before I talk about what the northerly and southerly routes are, I will explain some terminology. (i) There are light and darkness; the light is the deity of Fire, which is also called *Arciḥ* (अर्चिः) in the Vedic language. Smoke is the symbol of darkness; *Dhūma* (धूम) is the deity of smoke. (ii) A day consisting of 24 hours is divided into two – day and night; there is a deity of day and a deity of night. (iii) Based on the

---

[1] *Śrīmad Bhagavad Gītā Tattvavivecanī* by Jayadayal Goyandka (see Bibliography) has given an explicit explanation of these terms in the commentary on Verses 23 to 25 of Chapter VIII.

lunar calendar, a month is divided into two – bright fortnight and dark fortnight. The bright fortnight consists of the 14 days of the waxing moon, which is called *Śukla-Pakṣa* (शुक्लपक्ष). The dark fortnight is the 14 days of the waning moon, which is addressed as *Kṛṣṇa-Pakṣa* (कृष्णपक्ष); both *Śukla-Pakṣa* and *Kṛṣṇa-Pakṣa* have their deities. (iv) A year consists of two periods, one when the sun travels northwards, and the other when it travels southwards. The period when the sun goes for six months northwards is known as *Uttarāyaṇa* (उत्तरायण), whereas the period of the sun's southward journey for six months is called *Dakṣināyaṇa* (दक्षिणायण). Both *Uttarāyaṇa* and *Dakṣināyaṇa* have their own deities. (v) The year, sun, moon, lightning, and sky have their own presiding gods. The deity of the sun is called *Āditya* (आदित्य), and that of the moon is addresses as *Candra* (चन्द्र), who is also known as King *Soma* (सोम). The god of the sky or space is known as *Ākāśa* (आकाश). There is also a region of manes, which is called *Pitṛloka* (पितृलोक).

Northern Path

There is a yogĩ, who has known *Brahman* by reading scriptures and with the grace of his guru. However, he has not yet realized *Brahman*, meaning he has not yet reached the state of *Jivanmukta*. The soul of such yogĩ travels by the northern path. Such yogī does not return to the world; instead, he attains *Brahman*.

According to the *Chāndogya Upaniṣad* (छान्दोग्य उपनिषद्) IV.15.5 and V.10.1-2, the soul of such yogi first goes to the light (the deity of fire); from there it goes to [the god of] day. From [the god of] day it goes to [the deity of the] bright fortnight, and then to [the god of] the six-month period when the sun travels northwards. Afterwards, it goes to [the deity of] year. From [the deity of] year, it goes one by one to [the abodes of the deities of] the sun, moon, and lightning. Then a transcendental person comes and helps him to attain *Brahman*.

This path is called the path of gods because various deities or gods help him at every step; it is also known as the path of *Brahman* because this path finally takes the aspirant to attain *Brahman*.

Obviously, the person who meditates on the fourth *mātrā*, after death, travels by the northern path and never returns to the earth again.

The reader must understand that the Self-realized yogī, who has attained *mokṣha* (liberation) in this very life, is called *jivan-mukta* (जीवन्मुक्त). He has already realized that he is *Brahman*, the Ultimate Reality. After death, he does not travel by any of the paths, because he is already liberated; he has attained immortality. Such yogī has attained *Kaivalya mokṣa* (कैवल्य मोक्ष). According to the *Muṇḍaka Upaniṣad* (मुण्डक उपनिषद्) III.2.9, whoever knows the supreme *Brahman* becomes the very *Brahman*. Here, the word 'knows' refers to the actual realization of *Brahman*.

Southern Path

A person who has performed meritorious deeds, such as, performing *yajñas* (यज्ञ) and charitable works, and helping and protecting oppressed and less fortunate people, etc., takes the southern path.

According to the *Chāndogya Upaniṣad* V.10.3-5, such person, after death, goes to *Dhūma* [the deity of smoke] from where he goes to [the god of] night. Then he goes to [the deity of] the dark fortnight, and from there to [the deity of] the six-month period when the sun travels southwards.

He does not go to [the deity of the] year; instead, he directly goes to the region of manes. From there, he goes to *Ākāśa* [the deity of sky or space], then to [the god of] the moon.

He lives in the region of the moon until all the fruits of his karmas [actions] have exhausted. Then he returns to the world. Here, the region of the moon is equivalent to heaven (*Svarga-Loka* स्वर्गलोक).

After returning from the abode of the god of the moon, such a person may go through many cycles of births and deaths before proceeding on the northern path, or he may become *jīvan-mukta*, meaning he may attain liberation while he is still alive. The *Yoga-bhraṣṭa* (योगभ्रष्ट) yogīs, meaning the advanced yogīs, who die before actually knowing *Brahman*, as mentioned in the *Bhagavad Gītā* VI.41– also take the southern path. Then, they return to the world to continue their spiritual journey.

The reader should note that the soul of the person who has performed mostly villainous actions, and maybe some virtuous actions, does not travel by these two paths; instead, it directly goes to hell to suffer. After most of his vicious actions are exhausted, he returns to the world to bear the fruits of his remaining noble and malicious actions. He gets another chance to perform meritorious actions or spiritual penance so that he can travel by the two paths – northern or southern.

Praśna Upaniṣad (प्रश्न उपनिषद्) I.9-10 gives a similar idea:

> The year is indeed *Prajāpati* having two paths – southern and northern. Those who perform Vedic *yajñas*, philanthropic works, and charitable deeds – believing these deeds are of the supreme value – go to the region of the moon and then come back to this world. *Ṛṣis* (ऋषि), meaning sages, who desire to have their progeny, go by the southern path. This is the path of manes ||9||
>
> But those who seek *Ātman* (i.e., *Brahman*), through austerity, chastity, faith, veneration, and spiritual knowledge go to the abode of the sun taking the northern path. The dwelling of the sun is the storehouse of all energy, it is

nectar, free from fear, and the final place of refuge. From there they do not return ||10||

According to *Śrīmad Bhagavad Gītā* VIII.23-25, *Śrī Kṛṣṇa* is telling Arjuna:

यत्र काले त्वनावृत्तिमावृत्तिं चैव योगिनः |
प्रयाता यान्ति तं कालं वक्ष्यामि भरतर्षभ ||
Yatra kāle tvanāvṛtti - māvṛttiṁ caiva yoginaḥ |
Prayātā yānti taṁ kālaṁ vakṣyāmi bharatarṣabha ||23||

Arjuna, I will tell you the time at which the yogīs, after departing from this world, do or do not return.

अग्निर्ज्योतिरहः शुक्लः षण्मासा उत्तरायणम् |
तत्र प्रयाता गच्छन्ति ब्रह्म ब्रह्मविदो जनाः ||
Agnir-jyotirahaḥ śuklaḥ ṣaṇmāsā uttarāyaṇam |
Tatra prayātā gacchanti brahma brahma-vido janāḥ ||24||

The knowers of *Brahman* attain *Brahman* [and do not return to the world] when they depart from the world during the influence of effulgent fire, and during the day, the bright fortnight, and six months of the northward course of the sun.

धूमो रात्रिस्तथा कृष्णः षण्मासा दक्षिणायनम् |
तत्र चान्द्रमसं ज्योतिर्योगी प्राप्य निवर्तते ||
Dhūmo rātris-tathā kṛṣṇaḥ ṣaṇmāsā dakṣiṇāyanam |
Tatra Cāndramasaṁ jyotir - yogī prāpya nivartate ||25||

> When the yogī departs during the influence of smoke at night during the dark fortnight and the six months of the southward journey of the sun, he reaches the light of the moon and then comes back.

If we go by the literal meaning of these verses, it appears that these two paths are related to the timings at which the yogīs die, irrespective of how much spiritually advanced they are. It does not make sense. Therefore, to understand these verses, we must refer to the explanation given below.

Śrīmad Bhagavad Gītā Tattvavivecanī by Jayadayal Goyandka (see Bibliography) very beautifully explains these verses; I will summarize it. When a knower of *Brahman*, [who is almost a *Jivan-mukta*, but has not yet attained the state of liberation in this very life], dies during the daytime of the bright fortnight when the sun travels northwards, he directly moves on the northern path. However, if he dies at night, his soul stays with the deity of the day until it is the daytime, and then he proceeds on the northern path. If he dies during the dark fortnight of the waning moon, his soul stays with the deity of the bright fortnight of the waxing moon until the bright fortnight comes, and then he proceeds on the northern path. If he dies during the six months when the sun moves southwards, his soul stays with the deity of the six months of the sun's northward journey, and when the sun starts traveling northwards, he proceeds on the northern path.

Similarly, when a person, who has performed meritorious deeds, dies at night during the dark fortnight of the waning moon when the sun is on the southward course, he directly travels on the southern path. However, if he dies during the day, his soul stays with the deity of the night until it is the nighttime, and then he proceeds on the southern path. If he dies during the bright fortnight of the waxing moon, his soul stays with the deity of the dark fortnight of the waning moon until the dark fortnight comes, and then he proceeds on the southern path. If he dies during the six months when the sun is on the northward journey, his soul stays with the deity of the six months of the sun's southward journey, and when the sun starts traveling southwards, he proceeds on the southern path.

5.11 [1]**वालाग्रमात्रं हृदयस्थ मध्ये विश्वं देवं जातरूपं वरेण्यम् | तमात्मस्थं ये नु पश्यन्ति धीरास्तेषां शान्तिर्भवति नेतरेषाम् |**

Vālāgra-mātraṁ hṛdayastha madhye viśvaṁ devaṁ jātarūpaṁ vareṇyam | Tamātmasthaṁ ye nu paśyanti dhīrās-teṣāṁ śāntitr-bhavati netareṣām |

> The all-pervading, splendid, adorable Divine Being dwelling within the heart is as subtle as the end of a hair. Only those steadfast wise

---

[1] बालाग्रमात्रं हृदयस्य मध्ये विश्वं देवं वह्निरूपं वरेण्यम् |
तमात्मस्थं येऽनुपश्यन्ति धीरास्तेषां शान्तिः शाश्वती नेतरेषाम् || Linga II.18.34
Bālāgra-mātraṁ hṛdayasya madhye viśvaṁ devaṁ vahni-rūpaṁ vareṇyam |
Tamātma-sthaṁ ye'nupaśyanti dhīrās-teṣāṁ śantiḥ śāśvatī netareṣām ||

> men who indeed see Him within themselves attain the supreme peace, not others.

Vālāgra-mātram – *Vāla* or *Bāla* means hair, *agra* means front, *mātram* means measure; the phrase means one having the size of the end of a hair. Of course, the Supreme Being has no form or dimensions; He is subtler than the subtlest, he has no size, so, He cannot be measured.

Jāta-rūpam – brilliant, splendid, beautiful.

5.12 यस्मिन् क्रोधं याञ्च तृष्णां क्षमाञ्चाक्षमां हित्वा हेतुजालस्य मूलम् । बुद्ध्या सञ्चितं स्थापयित्वा तु रुद्रे रुद्रमेकत्वमाहुः ।

Yasmin krodhaṁ yāñca tṛṣṇāṁ kṣamāñcā-kṣamāṁ hitvā hetu-jālasya mūlam | Buddhyā sañcitaṁ sthāpayitvā tu rudre rudra-mekatva-māhuḥ |

> [The aspirant], who gets rid of anger, desires, forgiveness as well as non-forgiveness, which are the root cause of all bondage, [by destroying ignorance], and by mentally surrendering [all] accumulated [deeds, good as well as bad] to Lord Rudra, is said to become one with Lord Rudra.

Hetu-jālasya mūlam – *hetu* means the cause, *jāla* means net or binding, and *mūlam* means basis; thus, the phrase means the root cause of all binding.

There are five impediments in the path of spiritual progress – desire (*kāma* काम), anger (*krodha* क्रोध), greed (*lobha* लोभ), delusion or attachment (*moha* मोह), and ego (*ahaṅkāra* अहङ्कार). These impediments bind the individual to the world. The aspirant or the seeker of the Truth, with practice, must conquer these five impediments to attain his goal.

According to the mantra, *krodha* (anger), *tṛṣṇā* (desire), *kṣamā* (forgiveness), and *akṣamā* (non-forgiveness) are the cause of binding. When we talk of desire and anger, the other three impediments – greed, delusion, and ego – automatically become part of them. Forgiveness and non-forgiveness are part of the ego. Happiness and sufferings are the results of our own past actions. When someone gives us pleasure or pain, he is only a medium. It is our own past deeds which result in our happiness and misery. Who are we to forgive anyone? It is because of our ego we think we forgive or not forgive someone.

There are two ways to burn the past actions: (i) by experiencing (*bhoga* भोग) the results of those actions, and (ii) by the grace (*anugraha* अनुग्रह) of God. God bestows grace when the aspirant performs spiritual practices. The new deeds do not turn into results (i) when they are done for the benefit of the needy, without any selfish motive, or they are performed only for the sake of actions as a duty, and (ii) when they are surrendered to God.

The actions of a self-realized yogī, who is established in the Self or *Ātman*, do not bear fruits because he does not identify himself with the body-mind-ego; he is free from the five impediments. All his actions are performed by the body-mind-ego, which are part of nature, he has nothing to do with them. Of course, such a yogī will never perform any wrong actions. Since he does not get engaged in any fruit-bearing karma, he is not bound by them; he is ever free.

5.13 रुद्रो हि शाश्वतेन वै पुराणेनेषमूर्जेण तपसा नियन्ताग्निरिति भस्म वायुरिति भस्म जलमिति भस्म स्थलमिति भस्म व्योमेति भस्म सर्वं ह वा इदं भस्म मन एतानि चक्षूंषि यस्मादव्रतमिदं पाशुपतं यद्-भस्म नाङ्गानि संस्पृशेत् तस्माद्-ब्रह्म तदेतत् पाशुपतं पशुपाशविमोक्षणाय ॥ ५॥

Rudro hi śāśvatena vai purāṇeneṣa-mūrjeṇa tapasā niyantāgni-riti bhasma vāyuriti bhasma jalamiti bhasma sthalamiti bhasma vyometi bhasma sarvaṁ ha vā idaṁ bhasma mana etānni cakṣūṁṣi yasmāda-vrata-midaṁ pāśupataṁ yad-bhasma nāṅgāni saṁspṛśet tasmād-brahma tadetat pāśupataṁ paśupāśa-vimokṣaṇāya ||5||

Indeed, Rudra, through His austerity and vigor, which is eternal, ancient, and of nourishing nature, maintains the world.

Fire, air, water, earth, and space are *bhasma* (ashes), all this is indeed *bhasma*. A person who does not practice the rites of *Pāśupata Śaivism* and does not smear ashes on his body limbs, his mind, eyes, [and all sense-organs]

> are like ashes (meaning purposeless). Therefore, to be free from the worldly bondage, [the aspirant must follow] the *Pāśupata* rites, [which are like worshipping] *Brahman*. ||5||

Iṣa – *Iṣa* means juicy, fertile, possessing sap and strength, well-fed – it is nourishment. Lord Rudra provides nourishment or food and thus maintains the world (Note: the word *iṣa*, meaning nourishment or food, is different from *Īśa*, meaning ruler).

Ūrjeṇa – through vigor or energy; *Niyantā* – one who governs, maintains, or keeps order; *Bhasma* – ashes; it may also be interpreted as perishable.

Pāśupata – It is a *Śaivite* spiritual doctrine in which Śiva is addressed as *Paśupati*. In this practice, the Śiva devotee performs certain rites. One of the rituals is to apply *bhasma* (sacred ashes) to the body and wear *rudrākṣa mālā*, a rosary made of *rudrākṣa* beads. For staunch *Pāśupata* followers, the ashes could be from a human pyre. Ash is a symbol of detachment and renunciation. Since Hindus burn bodies after death, ashes remind us that no one can escape death.

Significance of *Bhasma*

Bhasma is not ordinary ashes; it is the left-over ashes from *yajña*, a sacrificial fire; or it is made from cow-dung following certain procedures reciting Vedic mantras. That is why it is also called '*vibhūti*' (विभूति), meaning glory, splendor, opulence, etc. *Vibhūti* is very auspicious and holy – it purifies the mind and brings blissfulness in life; it has healing and spiritual powers. *Bhasma* is also called *Rakṣā* (रक्षा) in Sanskrit or *Rākh* (राख) in Hindi because it protects the devotee from negative forces.

The *bhasma* generated from various substances, such as iron, gold, pearl, diamond, etc., is used as medicine in *Āyurveda*, Indian alternative medicine. It is beneficial for many diseases.

A Śiva devotee applies *bhasma* to his forehead by drawing three horizontal lines, called *tripuṇḍra* (त्रिपुण्ड्र). He may also draw *tripuṇḍra* on his chest, arms, legs, etc. A staunch devote, e.g., the follower of *Pāśupata* doctrine, smears *bhasma* on his whole body. '*Agni-riti bhasma*, *vāyuriti bhasma*, *jalamiti bhasma*, *sthalamiti bhasma*, *vyometi bhasma*, *sarvaṁ ha vā idaṁ bhasma*' – this is the *Pāśupata* hymn. The devotee, while reciting this hymn or some other mantras, applies ashes to his body.

When we say 'the fire, air, water, earth, and space are *bhasma* (ashes), all this is indeed *bhasma*,' what it means is that everything in this world gets destroyed, nothing is permanent. When the sun of our solar system will disintegrate after billions of years, all our planets, including the earth, will burn. In fact, at the time of the great dissolution (*Mahā-pralaya* महाप्रलय), the whole world will get destroyed. Only Lord Śiva or *Brahman*, who is eternal, will remain.

Bhasma reminds the aspirant that he must seek Śiva, the *Paramātman* – the Supreme Self – with his mind completely detached from this impermanent world.

Pāśupata Doctrine

Literally, *paśu* means an animal, *pāśa* means the rope which binds animals. All living beings (*jīvas*) and even the gods (*devas*) are considered as *paśus* because all are bound by the shackles of Śiva's Māyā to this impermanent *saṁsāra* (world). *Paśupati* means the Lord of *paśus*. Lord Śiva is known as *Paśupati*. Without Lord Śiva's grace, no one gets free from these shackles – the cycles of births and deaths.

|| Thus, ends Mantra 5 ||

||  ||

Mantra 6

This mantra is the prayer to Lord Rudra.

6.1 योऽग्नौ रुद्रो योऽप्स्वन्तर्य ओषधीर्वीरुध आविवेश। य इमा विश्वा भुवनानि चक्लृपे तस्मै रुद्राय नमोऽस्त्वग्नये।

Yo'gnau Rudro yo'psvantarya oṣadhīr-vīrudha āviveśa | *Ya imā viśvā bhuvanāni caklṛpe tasmai Rudrāya namo'stvagnaye* |

> Rudra, who is present in fire and water, has [also] entered herbs and plants. Prostrations to Rudra in the form of *Agni* (Fire-god), who has become all these worlds.

Yo'psvantar – This can be broken as '*yo apsu antar*' or '*yaḥ apsu antar*,' meaning one who is present in waters. In general, *ap* (अप्), meaning water, is used in the plural.

Oṣadhīr-vīrudha – *Oṣadhī* means medicines and herbs, and *vīrudha* stands for plants and shrubs.

Rudra is present in fire (*Agni* अग्नि) as well as water (*āpaḥ* आप:). There is nothing in the world that is without the presence of Rudra. The whole universe is pervaded by the

Supreme Consciousness, which is called *Cit Śakti* (चित् शक्ति) of Śiva. Śiva is the Ultimate Reality, *Saccidānanda* (सच्चिदानन्द). The word *Saccidānanda* can be broken as *Sat-Cit-Ānanda* (सत्-चित्-आनन्द), meaning Existence-Consciousness-Bliss.

Cakḷpe – *Cḷp* (कॢप्) means to create, produce, regulate, become, etc. *Cakḷpe* means 'has become;' all the worlds are a manifestation of Rudra.

6.2 यो रुद्रोऽग्नौ यो रुद्रोऽप्स्वन्तर्यो रुद्र ओषधीर्वीरुध आविवेश । यो रुद्र इमा विश्वा भुवनानि चक्लृपे तस्मै रुद्राय वै नमो नमः ।

Yo Rudro'gnau yo Rudro'psvantar-yo Rudra oṣadhīr-vīrudha āviveśa | Yo Rudra imā viśvā bhuvanāni cakḷpe tasmai Rudrāya vai namo namaḥ |

> Rudra, who is present in fire and water, has [also] entered medicines and plants. Again, and again, prostrations to Rudra, who has become all these worlds.

6.3 यो रुद्रोऽप्सु यो रुद्र ओषधीषु यो रुद्रो वनस्पतिषु ।

Yo Rudro'psu yo Rudra oṣadhīṣu yo Rudro vanaspatiṣu |

> Rudra, who is present in water, is [also] present in herbs and vegetation.

Śvetāśvatara Upaniṣad, Chapter II.17 has a similar mantra:

यो देवो अग्नौ योऽप्सु यो विश्वं भुवनमाविवेश ।
य ओषधीषु यो वनस्पतिषु तस्मै देवाय नमो नमः ॥

Yo devo agnau yo'psu yo viśvaṁ bhuvana-māviveśa |
ya oṣadhīṣu yo vanaspatiṣu tasmai devāya namo namaḥ||

> Prostration to that Divinity again and again who dwells in the fire, water, herbs, and vegetation, and who has entered the whole world.

6.4 येन रुद्रेण जगदूर्ध्वं धारितं पृथिवी द्विधा त्रिधा धर्त्ता धारिता नागा येऽन्तरिक्षे तस्मै रुद्राय वै नमो नमः ।

Yena Rudreṇa jagadūrdhvaṁ dhāritaṁ pṛthivī dvidhā tridhā dharttā dhāritā nāgā ye'ntarikṣe tasmai Rudrāya vai namo namaḥ |

> Prostrations to that Rudra, again and again, who, through His two-fold energy [Śiva and *Śakti*] and the three-fold nature [three *guṇas* or modes of nature] supports the world above (i.e., heaven), sustains the earth, and takes care of the *Nāgās* who live in the atmosphere.

Dvidhā – It means two-fold. It refers to the two energies of Śiva – Śiva and *Śakti* (शक्ति). *Śakti*, meaning energy or strength, is not different from Śiva, it is part of Śiva. Śiva, with the help of His *Śakti*, creates, maintains, and annihilates the world. *Dvidhā* may also refer to *Puruṣa* and *Prakṛti*. Śiva manifests Himself as *Puruṣa* and *Prakṛti*. *Puruṣa* is Consciousness, and *Prakṛti* is nature. The manifested universe is the combination of Consciousness as well as material nature.

Tridhā – It means three-fold. Human nature is three-fold; it consists of three *guṇas* (गुण) or three modes of nature. They are – (i) *Sattva* (सत्त्व) – goodness, purity, (ii) *Rajas* (रजस्) – passion, activity, and (iii) *Tamas* (तमस्) – ignorance, darkness, lethargy. In general, every human being has all these *guṇas*. A saintly person possesses more *sattva-guṇa* compared to *rajas, and tamas,* whereas an active person has more *rajas* than *sattva* and *tamas*. A vicious person has more *tamas* than *sattva* and *rajas*. A highly spiritual person transcends these three *guṇas* or modes of nature.

Śiva, through His Māyā (*Śakti*), consisting of the three *guṇas* – *Sattva*, *Rajas*, and *Tamas* – creates the world, and then sustains and protects it.

Nāgās – *Nāgās* are semidivine beings who are half humans and half serpents.

6.5 मूर्धानमस्य संसेव्याप्यथर्वा हृदयञ्च यत् । मस्तिष्कादूर्ध्वं प्रेरयत्यवमानोऽधिशीर्षतः । तद्वा अथर्वणः शिरो देवकोशः समुज्झितः । तत्प्राणोऽभिरक्षति शिरोऽन्तमथो मनः ।

Mūrdhāna-masya saṁsevyā-pyatharvā hṛdayañca yat | Mastiṣkā-dūrdhvaṁ prerayatyava-māno'dhi-

śīrṣataḥ | Tadvā Atharvaṇaḥ śiro devakośaḥ samujjhitaḥ | Tat-prāṇo'bhi-rakṣati śiro'ntamatho manaḥ |

> The steadfast yogī attains the highest goal [of realizing God] when he worships *Praṇava* (meaning OM), the crown over the top of Lord Rudra's head. One who disrespects [*Praṇava*], falls from the goal [of gaining spiritual wisdom]. The head of the steadfast yogī is left with the divine powers. The vital air, along with the peaceful mind, protects that head.

Atharvā – He was an ancient sage to whom the *Atharva-Veda* was revealed. The verb *tharv* (थर्व्) means to go or move; *tharvā* (थर्वा) means flickering, moving, or unsteady. *Atharvā* (अथर्वा) is the opposite of *tharvā*; Atharvā means steadfast or firm; it applies to yogīs. Since this part of the mantra applies to any sincere aspirant, I have translated the word *Atharvā* as the steadfast yogī, instead of Sage *Atharvā*.

Mūrdhāna – It means crown; *Praṇava* or OM is the crown of Lord Śiva's head.

Hṛdaya – Generally, it means heart, but it also means divine knowledge, science, or the best of anything. I have translated it as the highest goal, which is the best of everything. The highest goal is to realize God.

Prerayati – incites, directs, sends, inspires; *Avamāna* – disrespect or dishonor; *Adhi- śīrṣataḥ* – from the top of the head.

Samujjhita – abandoned, resigned, renounced, free from, that which is left, remnant, emit, drop, give out, pour down.

Prerayati avamāna adhi-śīrṣataḥ – It means one who dishonors [*Praṇava* or OM], falls from the top (i.e., goal).

Devakośa – It means the treasure box of gods (*devas*). It refers to the divine powers of gods. The steadfast yogī possesses the divine powers of all the gods.

Antamatho manaḥ – *Math* (मथ्) means to stir, whirl, churn. *Matho-manah* (मथोमन:) means churned mind; *anta* (अन्त) means the end. When the mind is churned, introspected, and analyzed, then its impurities go away, and what you have is a pure, quiet mind. Therefore, I have translated *Antamatho manaḥ* as a peaceful mind.

A yogī can protect his divine powers (head) by regulating the *prāṇa* (प्राण), the vital air, by practicing *prāṇāyāma* (प्राणायाम). He can also tame his mind through introspection, self-analysis, and meditation.

Here is a fascinating part. The Atharva-Veda *Saṁhitā*, mantras 10/2/26-27 say:

मूर्धानमस्य संसीव्याथर्वा हृदयञ्च यत्।
मस्तिष्कादूर्ध्वः प्रैरयत् पवमानोऽधि शीर्षतः ॥२६॥
तद्वा अथर्वणः शिरो देवकोशः समुब्जितः ।

तत्प्राणो अभिरक्षति शिरो अन्नमथो मनः ॥२७॥

Mūrdhāna-masya saṁsīvyā-tharvā hṛdayañca yat |
Mastiṣkā-dūrdhvaḥ prairayat pavamāno'dhi -śīrṣataḥ
||26||
Tadvā Atharvaṇaḥ śiro devakośaḥ samubjitaḥ |
Tat prāṇo abhirakṣati śiro annamatho manaḥ
||27||

The steadfast yogī uniting his head (intellect) and heart (emotions), impels the *prāṇa* (the vital air) in the head above the brain. The steadfast yogī's head is verily the well-guarded treasure of divine powers. The vital air, along with food and noble thoughts, protects that head.

Let us see the differences between the mantras of the *Atharva-Śira Upaniṣat* and the Atharva-Veda *Saṁhitā*:

- The former uses the word *saṁsevya*, meaning by serving or worshipping, whereas the latter is using the term *saṁsīvya*, meaning sewing together, which I have translated as uniting.

- In the former mantra, the word *hṛdaya* means the highest goal, whereas in the latter mantra it means the heart, the usual meaning.

- The former uses the word *avamāna*, meaning dishonor or disrespect, whereas the latter uses the word *pavamāna*, meaning *prāṇa* or the vital air.

- The former uses the word *samujjhita*, meaning left with, whereas the latter uses the word *samubjita*, meaning covered over – *Atharvā*'s head is covered with the treasure box of gods, which I have translated as the steadfast yogī's head is the well-guarded treasure of divine powers.

6.6 न च दिवो देवजनेन गुप्ता न चान्तरिक्षाणि न च भूम इमाः ।

Na ca divo deva-janena guptā na cāntarikṣāṇi na ca bhūma imāḥ |

> Gods (*devas*) themselves cannot protect heaven, earth, and the mid-region.

It is Rudra who protects everything.

6.7 यस्मिन्निदं सर्वमोतप्रोतं तस्मादन्यन्न परं किञ्चनास्ति । न तस्मात्पूर्वं न परं तदस्ति न भूतं नोत भव्यं यदासीत् । सहस्रपादेकमूर्ध्ना व्याप्तं स एवेदमावरीवर्ति भूतम् ।

Yasmin-nidaṁ sarva-motaprotaṁ tasmā-danyan-na paraṁ kiñcanāsti | Na tasmāt pūrvaṁ na paraṁ tadasti na bhūtaṁ nota bhavyaṁ yadāsīt | Sahasra-pādeka-mūrdhnā vyāptaṁ sa eveda-māvarīvarti bhūtam |

> All this [world] is interwoven within Him (i.e., within Rudra); there is nothing else superior to

> Him. Nothing ever indeed is, was, or will be superior to Him. He has one head and 1000 feet and pervades [the whole world], but at the same time, He remains concealed.

Otaprota – It means interwoven, extending in all directions. The whole world is interwoven within Rudra; there is nothing outside of Him.

Sahasra-pādeka-mūrdhnā – It means with one head and 1000 feet. Rudra is the head, which is one, and all the objects of the world are His numerous feet. Though He is one, He manifests as the multi-formed world. Also, as *Brahman*, He is one, but as *Ātman*, He dwells within every living being. As Consciousness (चेतनतत्त्व cetana-tattva), He pervades all.

Āvarīvarti – *Āvṛ* (आवृ) means to cover; *Āvarītṛ* (आवरीतृ) means one who veils or covers; *āvarīvarti* means remains covered or concealed. Concealing (*tirobhāva* तिरोभाव) Himself is one of the characteristics of Lord Śiva (see the commentary on Mantra 5.8); His vision is possible only with His grace (*anugraha* अनुग्रह).

6.8 अक्षरात् सञ्जायते कालः कालाद्-व्यापक उच्यते । व्यापको हि भगवान् रुद्रो भोगायमानो यदा शेते रुद्रस्तदा संहार्यते प्रजाः । उच्छ्वसिते तमो भवति तमस आपोऽश्वङ्गुल्या मथिते मथितं शिशिरे शिशिरं मथ्यमानं फेनं भवति फेनादण्डं भवत्यण्डाद्-ब्रह्मा भवति ब्रह्मणो वायुः

वायोरोङ्कार ओङ्कारात् सावित्री सावित्र्या गायत्री गायत्र्या लोका भवन्ति । अर्चयन्ति तपः सत्यं मधु क्षरन्ति यद्ध्रुवम् । एतद्धि परमं तपः । आपो ज्योती रसोऽमृतं ब्रह्म भूर्भुवःस्वरों नम इति ॥ ६॥

Akṣarāt sañjāyate kālaḥ kālād-vyāpaka ucyate | Vyāpako hi Bhagavān Rudro bhogāya-māno yadā śete Rudras-tadā saṁhāryate prjāḥ | Ucchvasite tamo bhavati tamasa āpo'śvaṅgulyā mathite mathitaṁ śiśire śiśiraṁ mathya-mānaṁ phenaṁ bhavati phenā-daṇḍaṁ bhavatyaṇḍād-Brahmā bhavati Brahmaṇo vāyuḥ vāyoroṅkāra Oṅkārāt Sāvitrī Sāvitryā Gāyatrī Gāyatryā lokā bhavanti | Arcayanti tapaḥ satyaṁ madhu kṣaranti yad-dhruvam | Etaddhi paramaṁ tapaḥ | Āpo jyotī raso'mṛtaṁ Brahma Bhūr-Bhuvaḥ Svaroṁ nama iti ||6||

From *Akṣara* (i.e., *Brahman*) is created *Kāla* (i.e., Time); it is said that He is all-pervading because of being *Kāla*. When all-pervading and delighted Lord Rudra sleeps, He withdraws all living beings [within Him]. When He breaths out, it becomes darkness; from darkness is created water; when the water is churned with finger, it shakes and becomes like the frost in winter; when stirred [further], it becomes foam; from the foam comes egg, from the egg *Brahmā*, from *Brahmā* the wind, from wind the sound Om, from the sound Om *Sāvitrī*, from *Sāvitrī Gāyatrī*, from *Gāyatrī* are born all the worlds (*Lokas* – for 14 *Lokas* or the worlds see the commentary on Mantra 2.14). [The seekers of Truth] worship austerity and truthfulness, which results in the constant flow of eternal nectar (ambrosia). This indeed is the supreme austerity; [this is] water, light, Rasa (Eternal Bliss), nectar, *Brahma*, earth, middle-region, heaven, and OM (or *Praṇava*). Obeisance to Him.

Akṣara – It means imperishable. *Brahman* (Absolute God), who is without any attributes and a form (निर्गुण-निराकार *Nirguṇa-Nirākāra*), is ever-existing. He is *niṣkriya* (निष्क्रिय inactive) and *akartā* (अकर्ता non-doer).

Kāla – Literally, it means time. Here, it refers to *Īśvara*, God with attributes but without a form (सगुण-निराकार *Saguṇa-Nirākāra*), who, with His Māyā, the illusory power, creates, sustains, and annihilates the world. When God destroys the world, He is called *Kāla* (काल), the annihilator. God is also called *Akāla* (अकाल), meaning God is beyond time; *Akāla* is the opposite of *Kāla*. When the world vanishes, the time disappears, but God always remains, and therefore, He is called *Akāla*. God is omnipresent and ever-present. His existence is not affected by time.

Rudra – Here, the word Rudra refers to *Īśvara* (ईश्वर), God with attributes, but without shape or form. When He sleeps, He withdraws all living beings within Him, meaning it is the annihilation of the world. His outward breath causes darkness. Before the creation of the world, there was only darkness all over.

Śiśira – The word has two meanings, winter, and frost (or dew). In winter, water in the air becomes frost or dew.

Sāvitrī and *Gāyatrī* – They are names of goddesses. *Gāyatrī* is also a powerful mantra. *Gāyatrī* is also a meter of poetry that has three *Pādas* (feet), each *Pāda* has 8 *mātrās* or syllables (see the commentary on Mantra 2.14 for the explanation).

Āpo jyotī raso'mṛtaṁ Brahma Bhūr-Bhuvaḥ-Svaḥ Om – All these words refer to *Brahman*. God is *āpaḥ* – God is water – because life cannot form and survive without water. God is *jyoti*, meaning light; it is God's brilliance present in suns and stars that shines the world. Light also refers to knowledge; God is the knowledge. The literal meaning of *Rasa* is a flavory juice which is most tasty, but here it relates to the Supreme Bliss. The Vedas say, '*Raso vai saḥ*' – He (meaning *Brahman*) is *Rasa*, the Eternal Supreme Bliss. God is also called *Sat-Cit-Ānanda* – Existence, Consciousness, and Bliss; thus, here *Rasa* means Bliss. The 14 worlds (see the commentary on Mantra 2.14) known as *Bhūr-Bhuvaḥ-Svaḥ,* etc., are God's manifestation. OM – there is no difference between *Brahman* and the syllable OM or the sound OM.

Per *Taittirīya Upaniṣad* II.1, from *Ātman* (*Brahman*) is born space; from space, the air is born; from the air, the fire takes place; from fire, water; from water comes the earth; from the earth, herbs; from herbs, food; from food, man. Per this mantra (Mantra 6.8), from the darkness came the water. Here, only the water is mentioned; space, air, and fire are skipped. This is to emphasize that it is the water from which life has evolved. Scientifically too, the presence of water is essential for life to form and sustain.

Chapter II of the *Matsya Purāṇa* (मत्स्य पुराण) says, "At the time of great dissolution of the universe when there was nothing but darkness, un-manifest and self-born *Brahman* tore the darkness and appeared as *Nārāyaṇa* (नारायण). *Nārāyaṇa* first created water and put His seed in it. From that seed was formed an egg. *Nārāyaṇa* entered that egg and spread within it. Thus, He is known as *Viṣṇu* (note: the root word of *Viṣṇu* is *viṣ*, which means to pervade). From that egg appeared *Sūrya* (सूर्य), the Sun-god, who came to be known as *Brahmā* (ब्रह्मा), who recited the Vedas. Then *Brahmā* created the world."

In this regard, one can see some similarities between the *Atharvaśira Upaniṣat* and the *Matsya Purāṇa*; here is the sequence of occurrences: dissolution → darkness → water → egg → *Brahmā* → the world.

|| Thus, ends Mantra 6 ||

फलश्रुतिः

Phalaśrutiḥ

(Fruits of Reciting *Atharvaśira Upaniṣat*)

य इदमथर्वशिरो ब्राह्मणोऽधीते। अश्रोत्रियः श्रोत्रियो भवति। अनुपीत उपनीतो भवति। सोऽग्निपूतो भवति। स वायुपूतो भवति। स सूर्यपूतो भवति। स सोमपूतो भवति। स सत्यपूतो भवति। स सर्वपूतो भवति।

Ya idama-tharvaśiro brāhmaṇo'dhīte | Aśrotriyaḥ śrotriyo bhavati | Anupanīta upanīto bhavati | So'gnipūto bhavati | Sa vāyupūto bhavati | Sa sūryapūto bhavati | Sa somapūto bhavati | Sa satyapūto bhavati | Sa sarvapūto bhavati |

When a Brahmin studies this *Atharvaśira*, he becomes well conversant with the Vedas, if he is already not so. [By studying *Atharvaśira*], one gets initiated into the twice-born class (Brahmins, warriors, and business people) if he is not already so. He gets purified by [the grace of] *Agni* (Fire-god), *Vāyu* (Air-god – wind), the Sun-god, and the Moon-god. He gets purified

> like those who follow the path of Truth. He gets purified in all respects.

Aśrotriyaḥ śrotriyo bhavati –Literally, *Śruti* means that which is heard. In ancient times, students learned Vedas and *Upaniṣads* by listening to them from their guru, and that is why the Vedas and *Upaniṣads* are called *Śruti*. *Śrotriya* means one who is conversant with the sacred knowledge of *Śruti*. *Śrotriyas* are called Brahmins. The *Atharvaśira Upaniṣat* is recited as the worship part of the Vedas, and it is studied to understand the supreme philosophy of the *Upaniṣads*. Therefore, by just reciting and studying the *Atharvaśira*, one acquires all the collective knowledge of the Vedas and the *Upaniṣads*.

Anupanīta upanīto bhavati – *Upanīta* means initiated. When a child is about five years old, a ceremony is performed in which he wears a holy thread (*Upanayana*). Thus, he is initiated to the Student life, called *Brahmacarya Āśrama* (ब्रह्मचर्य आश्रम). After this initiation ceremony, the child is called twice-born (द्विज *dvija*), and then he is eligible to study the Vedas. Even if the aspirant was not initiated to the twice-born class by performing the thread ceremony, the study of the *Atharvaśira* makes him qualified for the Vedic learning.

The mantra further says that by just studying the *Atharvaśira Upaniṣat*, the person gets purified with the grace of all the gods.

स सर्वैर्-देवैर्ज्ञातो भवति । स सर्वैर्-वेदैरनुध्यातो भवति । स सर्वेषु तीर्थेषु स्नातो भवति । तेन सर्वैः क्रतुभिरिष्टं भवति । गायत्र्याः षष्टिसहस्राणि जप्तानि भवन्ति । इतिहास-पुराणानां रुद्राणां शतसहस्राणि जप्तानि भवन्ति । प्रणवानामयुतं जप्तं भवति । स चक्षुषः पङ्क्तिं पुनाति ।

Sa sarvair-devair jñāto bhavati | Sa sarvair-vedai-ranudhyāto bhavati | Sa sarveṣu tīrtheṣu snāto bhavati | Tena sarvaiḥ kratubhiriṣṭaṁ bhavati | Gāyatryāḥ ṣaṣṭi-sahasrāṇi japtāni bhavanti | Itihāsa-purāṇānāṁ rudrāṇāṁ śatasahasrāṇi japtāni bhavanti | Praṇavā-nāmayutaṁ japtaṁ bhavati | Sa cakṣuṣaḥ paṅktiṁ punāti ||

He becomes known to all gods and is meditated upon by all the Vedas. He obtains the fruits of taking a bath in the waters of all the holy places. He gets rewarded with the fruits of performing meritorious deeds like all types of *yajñas*, chanting the *Gāyatrī* mantra 60,000 times, studying all the epics and *Purāṇās*, repeating the Rudra mantras 100,000 times, and the *Praṇava* mantra (OM mantra) 10,000 times. [In fact,] all those whom he looks at are purified.

Sa sarvair-vedai-ranudhyāto bhavati – Saḥ sarvaiḥ vedaiḥ anudhyātaḥ bhavati: meaning he, the one who chants this

Upaniṣad, is meditated upon by all the Vedas. Here the Vedas are personified. Normally, the aspirants meditate upon the hymns of the Vedas, but in this case, the *Atharvaśira Upaniṣat* is so great that even the Vedas themselves meditate upon the one who recites it.

Gāyatrī mantra – For the explanation and significance of the Gāyatrī mantra, see the commentary on Mantra 2.14.

Epics and *Purāṇās* – There are two epics, *Rāmāyaṇa* (रामायण) and *Mahābhārata* (महाभारत). They are history books written in poetry. The *Rāmāyaṇa* was written by Sage *Vālmīki* (वाल्मीकि) and has 24,000 verses, whereas the *Mahābhārata*, which was written by Sage *Vedavyāsa* (वेदव्यास), has more than 100,000 verses.

There are 18 major and 18 minor *Purāṇas* (पुराण), written by Sage *Vedavyāsa*.

Rudra mantra: *Śatarudriya* (शतरुद्रिय), *Rudrāṣṭādhāyī* (रुद्राष्टाध्यायी), and *Rudra Praśna* (रुद्रप्रश्न) are some of the Rudra *Śastras* (शास्त्र sacred books) that give Rudra mantras.

आसप्तमात् पुरुषयुगान् पुनातीत्याह भगवानथर्वशिरः सकृज्जप्तैव शुचिः स पूतः कर्मण्यो भवति । द्वितीयं जप्त्वा गणाधिपत्यमवाप्नोति । तृतीयं जप्त्वैवमेवानुप्रविशत्यों सत्यमों सत्यमों सत्यम् । इत्यथर्ववेदे शिवाथर्वशीर्षम् ॥

Āsaptamāt puruṣa-yugān punātītyāha bhagavā-natharva-śiraḥ sakṛj-japtaiva śuciḥ sa pūtaḥ karmaṇyo bhavati | Dvitīyaṁ japtvā gaṇādhipatya-mavāpnoti | Tṛtīyaṁ japtvaiva-mevānu-praviśatyoṁ satyamoṁ satyamoṁ satyam | Ityatharva-vede Śivātharva- Śīrṣam ||

He purifies his ancestors from the past seven generations. The Lord said that when a person recites *Atharvaśira* once, he gets purified and becomes qualified to conduct religious rites. By chanting it the second time, he gets the seat of G*aṇapati*, who rules over *gaṇas* (i.e., devotees, who surround and serve Lord Śiva in *Śivaloka*). When he recites it the third time, he enters OM (i.e., *Brahman*) – OM is the Truth, the Ultimate Reality.

Thus, the *Śivātharva-Śīrṣa, which* is part of the *Atharva-Veda*, ends.

The highest goal of life is to get liberated and be free from the cycles of births and deaths. By just reciting the *Atharvaśira* three times, one attains *mokṣa*. It shows the importance of this sacred scripture.

|| इति शिर उपनिषत् ||

|| *Iti Śira Upaniṣat* ||

Thus, the discourse on the *Brahma-vidyā* ends.

Brahma-vidyā – It means the knowledge of *Brahman*, the Ultimate Reality; it is the supreme knowledge. By studying the *Atharvaśira Upaniṣat*, one acquires the highest knowledge.

|| शान्तिपाठः ||

|| *Śānti-Pāṭhaḥ* ||

Peace Chant

ॐ सह नाववतु । सह नौ भुनक्तु । सह वीर्यङ्करवावहै । तेजस्वि नावधीतमस्तु मा विद्विषावहै ॥

॥ ॐ शान्तिः शान्तिः शान्तिः ॥

Om Saha nāvavatu | Saha nau bhunaktu | Saha vīryaṅ-karavā-vahai | Tejasvi nā-vadhītamastu mā vidviṣā-vahai ||

|| *Om Śāntiḥ Śāntiḥ Śāntiḥ* ||

May He (*Brahman* – God) protect us both [the guru and the disciple], may He nourish us both, may we both work together with tremendous strength, may our study [of scriptures] be vibrant, may we not hate each other.

Peace, peace, peace!

॥ ॐ ॥

Sanskrit Text

[1]अथर्वशिर उपनिषत्
(शिवाथर्वशीर्षम्)

॥ शान्तिपाठः ॥

[2]ॐ भ॒द्द्रङ्कर्णे॑भिः शृणुयाम देवा भ॒द्द्रम्प॑श्श्येमा॒-
क्षभि॑र्य्यजत्राः। स्थि॒रैरङ्गै॑स्तुष्टु॒वाँ॑सस्त॒नूभि॒र्व्य॒शे-
महि दे॒वहि॑तं॒ यदायुः ॥

[1]*Atharvaśira Upaniṣat* is also known as *Śira-Upaniṣat*, *Atharva-Śīrṣam*, or *Śivātharva-Śīrṣam*. When it is recited in praise of Lord Śiva (in Śiva worship), it is commonly called *Śivātharva-Śīrṣam*. The Sanskrit text is mainly based on *Āhnika-Sūtra-valiḥ* (see Bibliography).

[2] *Śukla Yajurveda* 25-21

[1]ॐ स्वस्ति नऽइन्द्रो वृद्धश्श्रवाः स्वस्ति नः पूषा
व्विश्ववेदाः । स्वस्ति नस्तार्क्ष्योऽअरिष्टनेमिः
स्वस्ति नो बृहस्पतिर्द्दधातु ॥

ॐ सह नाववतु । सह नौ भुनक्तु । सह वीर्यङ्करवावहै ।
तेजस्वि नावधीतमस्तु मा विद्विषावहै ॥

॥ ॐ शान्तिः शान्तिः शान्तिः ॥

([2]कृष्णयजुर्वेदीय –

ॐ भद्रं कर्णेभिः शृणुयाम देवाः । भद्रं पश्येमा-
क्षभिर्यजत्राः । स्थिरैरङ्गैस्तुष्टुवाग्ं सस्तनूभिः । व्यशेम
देवहितं यदायुः ॥

ॐ स्वस्ति न इन्द्रो वृद्धश्रवाः । स्वस्ति नः पूषा
विश्ववेदाः । स्वस्ति नस्तार्क्ष्यो अरिष्टनेमिः ।
स्वस्ति नो बृहस्पतिर्दधातु ॥

---

[1] *Śukla Yajurveda* 25-19.

[2] *Taittirīya-Mantrakośaḥ* (see Bibliography)

ॐ सह नाववतु । सह नौ भुनक्तु । सह वीर्यं करवावहै । तेजस्वि नावधीतमस्तु मा विद्विषावहै ॥

॥ ॐ शान्तिः शान्तिः शान्तिः ॥)

॥ शिवाथर्वशीर्षम् ॥

अथ शिवाथर्वशीर्षम् (अथ शिर उपनिषत्) ॥ ॐ देवा ह वै स्वर्गलोकमायंस्ते रुद्रमपृच्छन् को भवानिति । सोऽब्रवीदहमेकः [1]प्रथममासोद्वर्तामि च भविष्यामि च नान्यः कश्चिन्मत्तो व्यतिरिक्त इति । सोऽन्तरादन्तरं प्राविशद्-दिशश्चान्तरं प्राविशत् सोऽहं नित्यानित्यो व्यक्ताव्यक्तो ब्रह्माब्रह्माहं प्राञ्चः प्रत्यञ्चोऽहं दक्षिणाञ्च उदञ्चोऽहमधश्चोर्ध्वश्चाहं दिशश्च प्रतिदिशश्चाहं पुमानपुमान् स्त्रियश्चाहं सावित्र्यहं गायत्र्यहं त्रिष्टुब्जगत्यनुष्टुप् चाऽहं छन्दोऽहं सत्योऽहं गार्हपत्यो दक्षिणाग्निराहवनीयोऽहं गौरहं गौर्यहमृगहं यजुरहं सामाहमथर्वाङ्गिरसोऽहं ज्येष्ठोऽहं श्रेष्ठोऽहं वरिष्ठोऽहमापोऽहं तेजोऽहं गुह्योऽहमरण्योऽहमक्षरमहं क्षरमहं पुष्करमहं पवित्रमहमुग्रञ्च [2]बलिश्च पुरस्ताज्-

---

[1] Alternative texts: प्रथममास वर्तामि or प्रथममासं वर्तामि

[2] Alternative text: बहिश्च

ज्योतिरित्यहमेव सर्वेभ्यो मामेव स सर्वः [1]समो यो मां वेद स देवान्वेद सर्वांश्च वेदान् साङ्गानपि ब्रह्म ब्राह्मणैश्च गां गोभिर्-ब्राह्मणान् ब्राह्मणेन हविर्हविषा आयुरायुषा सत्यं सत्येन धर्मेण धर्मं तर्पयामि स्वेन तेजसा। ततो ह वै ते देवा रुद्रमपृच्छन् ते देवा रुद्रमपश्यन् ते देवा रुद्रमध्यायन् ते देवा ऊर्ध्वबाहवो रुद्रं स्तुवन्ति ॥ १ ॥

ॐ यो वै रुद्रः स भगवान् यश्च ब्रह्मा तस्मै वै नमो नमः ।१॥
यो वै रुद्रः स भगवान् यश्च विष्णुस्तस्मै वै नमो नमः ।२॥
यो वै रुद्रः स भगवान् यश्च स्कन्दस्तस्मै वै नमो नमः ।३॥
यो वै रुद्रः स भगवान् यश्चेन्द्रस्तस्मै वै नमो नमः ।४॥
यो वै रुद्रः स भगवान् यश्चाग्निस्तस्मै वै नमो नमः ।५॥

यो वै रुद्रः स भगवान् यश्च वायुस्तस्मै वै नमो नमः ।६॥
यो वै रुद्रः स भगवान् यश्च सूर्यस्तस्मै वै नमो नमः ।७॥
यो वै रुद्रः स भगवान् यश्च सोमस्तस्मै वै नमो नमः ।८॥
यो वै रुद्रः स भगवान् ये चाष्टौ ग्रहास्तस्मै वै नमो नमः ।९॥
यो वै रुद्रः स भगवान् ये चाष्टौ प्रतिग्रहास्तस्मै वै नमो नमः ।१०॥

---

[1] Alternative texts: समायो or स मां यो

योवैरुद्रः स भगवान् यच्च भूस्तस्मै वै नमो नमः ॥११॥
यो वै रुद्रः स भगवान् यच्च भुवस्तस्मै वै नमो नमः ॥१२॥
यो वै रुद्रः स भगवान् यच्च स्वस्तस्मै वै नमो नमः ॥१३॥
यो वै रुद्रः स भगवान् यच्च महस्तस्मै वै नमो नमः ॥१४॥
यो वै रुद्रः स भगवान् या च पृथिवी तस्मै वै नमो नमः ॥१५॥

यो वै रुद्रः स भगवान् यच्चान्तरिक्षं तस्मै वै नमो नमः ॥१६॥
यो वै रुद्रः स भगवान् या च द्यौस्तस्मै वै नमो नमः ॥१७॥
यो वै रुद्रः स भगवान् याश्चापस्तस्मै वै नमो नमः ॥१८॥
यो वै रुद्रः स भगवान् यच्च तेजस्तस्मै वै नमो नमः ॥१९॥
यो वै रुद्रः स भगवान् यश्च कालस्तस्मै वै नमो नमः ॥२०॥

यो वै रुद्रः स भगवान् यश्च यमस्तस्मै वै नमो नमः ॥२१॥
यो वै रुद्रः स भगवान् यश्च मृत्युस्तस्मै वै नमो नमः ॥२२॥
यो वै रुद्रः स भगवान् यच्चामृतं तस्मै वै नमो नमः ॥२३॥
यो वै रुद्रः स भगवान् यच्चाकाशं तस्मै वै नमो नमः ॥२४॥
यो वै रुद्रः स भगवान् यच्च विश्वं तस्मै वै नमो नमः ॥२५॥

यो वै रुद्रः स भगवान् यच्च स्थूलं तस्मै वै नमो नमः ॥२६॥
यो वै रुद्रः स भगवान् यच्च सूक्ष्मं तस्मै वै नमो नमः ॥२७॥
यो वै रुद्रः स भगवान् यच्च शुक्लं तस्मै वै नमो नमः ॥२८॥
यो वै रुद्रः स भगवान् यच्च कृष्णं तस्मै वै नमो नमः ॥२९॥
यो वै रुद्रः स भगवान् यच्च कृत्स्नं तस्मै वै नमो नमः ॥३०॥

यो वै रुद्रः स भगवान् यच्च सत्यं तस्मै वै नमो नमः ।३१॥
यो वै रुद्रः स भगवान् यच्च सर्वं तस्मै वै नमो नमः ।३२॥२॥

भूस्ते आदिर्मध्यं भुवस्ते स्वस्ते शीर्षं विश्वरूपोऽसि ब्रह्मैकस्त्वं द्विधा त्रिधा वृद्धिस्त्वं शान्तिस्त्वं पुष्टिस्त्वं हुतमहुतं दत्तमदत्तं सर्वमसर्वं विश्वमविश्वं कृतमकृतं परमपरं परायणञ्च त्वम् । अपाम सोमममृता अभूमागन्म ज्योतिरविदाम देवान् । किं नूनमस्मान् कृणवदरातिः किमु धूर्तिरमृतं मर्त्यस्य । सोमसूर्यपुरस्तात् सूक्ष्मः पुरुषः । सर्वं जगद्धितं वा एतदक्षरं प्राजापत्यं सौम्यं सूक्ष्मं पुरुषं ग्राह्यमग्राह्येण भावं भावेन सौम्यं सौम्येन सूक्ष्मं सूक्ष्मेण वायव्यं वायव्येन ग्रसति तस्मै महाग्रासाय वै नमो नमः । हृदिस्था देवताः सर्वा हृदि प्राणाः प्रतिष्ठिताः । हृदि त्वमसि यो नित्यं तिस्रो मात्राः परस्तु सः । तस्योत्तरतः शिरो दक्षिणतः पादौ य उत्तरतः स ओङ्कारः य ओङ्कारः स प्रणवः यः प्रणवः स सर्वव्यापी यः सर्वव्यापी सोऽनन्तः योऽनन्तस्तत्तारं यत्तारं तच्छुक्लं यच्छुक्लं तत्सूक्ष्मं यत्सूक्ष्मं तद्वैद्युतं यद्वैद्युतं तत्परं ब्रह्म यत्परं ब्रह्म स एकः य एकः स रुद्रः यो रुद्रः स ईशानः य ईशानः स भगवान् महेश्वरः ॥ ३ ॥

अथ कस्मादुच्यते ओङ्कारः । यस्मादुच्चार्यमाण एव प्राणानूर्ध्वमुत्क्रामयति तस्मादुच्यते ओङ्कारः । अथ कस्मादुच्यते

प्रणवः यस्मादुच्चार्यमाण एव ऋग्यजुःसामाथर्वाङ्गिरसं ब्रह्म ब्राह्मणेभ्यः प्रणामयति नामयति च तस्मादुच्यते प्रणवः। अथ कस्मादुच्यते सर्वव्यापी यस्मादुच्चार्यमाण एव यथा स्नेहेन पललपिण्डमिव शान्तरूपमोतप्रोतमनुप्राप्तो व्यतिषक्तश्च तस्मादुच्यते सर्वव्यापी। अथ कस्मादुच्यतेऽनन्तः। यस्मादुच्चार्यमाण एव तिर्यगूर्ध्वमधस्ताच्चास्यान्तो नोपलभ्यते तस्मादुच्यतेऽनन्तः। अथ कस्मादुच्यते तारं यस्मादुच्चार्यमाण एव गर्भजन्मव्याधिजरामरणसंसार-महाभयात् तारयति त्रायते च तस्मादुच्यते तारम्। अथ कस्मादुच्यते शुक्लं यस्मादुच्चार्यमाण एव क्लन्दते क्लामयति च तस्मादुच्यते शुक्लम्। अथ कस्मादुच्यते सूक्ष्मं यस्मादुच्चार्यमाण एव सूक्ष्मो भूत्वा शरीराण्यधितिष्ठति सर्वाणि चाङ्गान्यभिमृश्यति तस्मादुच्यते सूक्ष्मम्। अथ कस्मादुच्यते वैद्युतम्। यस्मादुच्चार्यमाण एव व्यक्ते महति तमसि द्योतयति तस्मादुच्यते वैद्युतम्। अथ कस्मादुच्यते परं ब्रह्म यस्मात् परमपरं परायणञ्च बृहद्-बृहत्या बृंहयति तस्मादुच्यते परं ब्रह्म। अथ कस्मादुच्यते एकः यः सर्वान् प्राणान् सम्भक्ष्य सम्भक्षणेनाजः संसृजति विसृजति तीर्थमेके व्रजन्ति तीर्थमेके दक्षिणाः प्रत्यञ्च उदञ्चः प्राञ्चोऽभिव्रजन्त्येके तेषां सर्वेषामिह सङ्गतिः साकं स

[1]एकोऽभूदन्तश्चरति प्रजानां तस्मादुच्यते एकः । अथ कस्मादुच्यते रुद्रः यस्मादृषिभिर्-नान्यैर्-भक्तैर्-द्रुतमस्य रूपमुपलभ्यते तस्मादुच्यते रुद्रः । अथ कस्मादुच्यते ईशानः यः सर्वान् देवानीशते ईशानीभिर्-जननीभिश्च शक्तिभिः । अभित्वा शूर नो नुमो दुग्धा इव धेनवः । ईशानमस्य जगतः स्वर्दृशमीशानमिन्द्र तस्थुष इति तस्मादुच्यते ईशानः । अथ कस्मादुच्यते भगवान् महेश्वरः यस्माद्-भक्तान् ज्ञानेन भजत्यनुगृह्णाति च वाचं संसृजति विसृजति च सर्वान् भावान् परित्यज्यात्मज्ञानेन योगैश्वर्येण महति महीयते तस्मादुच्यते भगवान् महेश्वरः । तदेतद्-रुद्रचरितम् ॥४॥

एषो ह देवः प्रदिशोऽनु सर्वाः पूर्वो ह जातः स उ गर्भे अन्तः । स एव जातः स जनिष्यमाणः प्रत्यङ्जनास्तिष्ठति सर्वतोमुखः । एको रुद्रो न द्वितीयाय तस्मै य इमाँल्लोकानीशत ईशनीभिः । प्रत्यङ्जनास्तिष्ठति सञ्चुकोचान्तकाले संसृज्य विश्वा-भुवनानि गोप्ता । यो योनिं योनिमधितिष्ठत्येको येनेदं सर्वं विचरति सर्वम् । तमीशानं वरदं देवमीड्यं निचाय्येमां शान्तिमत्यन्तमेति । क्षमां हित्वा हेतुजालस्य मूलं बुद्ध्या सञ्चितं स्थापयित्वा तु रुद्रे । रुद्रमेकत्वमाहुः शाश्वतं वै

[1] Alternative text - एको भूतश्चरति

पुराणमिषमूर्जेण पशवोऽनुनामयन्तं मृत्युपाशान् । तदेतेनात्मन्नेतेनार्धचतुर्थेन मात्रेण शान्तिं संसृजति पशुपाशविमोक्षणम् । या सा प्रथमा मात्रा ब्रह्मदेवत्या रक्ता वर्णेन यस्तां ध्यायते नित्यं स गच्छेद्-ब्रह्मपदम् । या सा द्वितीया मात्रा विष्णुदेवत्या कृष्णवर्णेन यस्तां ध्यायते नित्यं स गच्छेद्-वैष्णवं पदम् । या सा तृतीया मात्रा ईशानदेवत्या कपिला वर्णेन यस्तां ध्यायते नित्यं स गच्छेदैशानं पदम् । या सार्धचतुर्थी मात्रा सर्वदेवत्याऽव्यक्तीभूता खं विचरति शुद्धा स्फटिकसन्निभा वर्णेन यस्तां ध्यायते नित्यं स गच्छेत् पदमनामयम् । तदेतदुपासीत मुनयो वाग्वदन्ति न तस्य ग्रहणमयं पन्था विहित उत्तरेण येन देवा यान्ति येन पितरो येन ऋषयः परमपरं परायणं चेति । वालाग्रमात्रं हृदयस्य मध्ये विश्वं देवं जातरूपं वरेण्यम् । तमात्मस्थं ये नु पश्यन्ति धीरास्तेषां शान्तिर्भवति नेतरेषाम् । यस्मिन् क्रोधं याञ्च तृष्णां क्षमाञ्चाक्षमां हित्वा हेतुजालस्य मूलम् । बुद्धया सञ्चितं स्थापयित्वा तु रुद्रे रुद्रमेकत्वमाहुः । रुद्रो हि शाश्वतेन वै पुराणेनेषमूर्जेण तपसा नियन्ताग्निरिति भस्म वायुरिति भस्म जलमिति भस्म स्थलमिति भस्म व्योमेति भस्म सर्वं ह वा इदं भस्म मन एतानि चक्षूंषि यस्मादव्रतमिदं पाशुपतं यद्-भस्म नाङ्गानि संस्पृशेत् तस्माद्-ब्रह्म तदेतत् पाशुपतं पशुपाशविमोक्षणाय ॥ ५॥

योऽग्नौ रुद्रो योऽप्स्वन्तर्य ओषधीर्वीरुध आविवेश । य इमा विश्वा भुवनानि चक्लृपे तस्मै रुद्राय नमोऽस्त्वग्नये । यो रुद्रोऽग्नौ यो रुद्रोऽप्स्वन्तर्यो रुद्र ओषधीर्वीरुध आविवेश । यो रुद्र इमा विश्वा भुवनानि चक्लृपे तस्मै रुद्राय वै नमो नमः । यो रुद्रोऽप्सु यो रुद्र ओषधीषु यो रुद्रो वनस्पतिषु । येन रुद्रेण जगदूर्ध्वं धारितं पृथिवी द्विधा त्रिधा धर्त्ता धारिता नागा येऽन्तरिक्षे तस्मै रुद्राय वै नमो नमः । मूर्धानमस्य संसेव्याप्यथर्वा हृदयञ्च यत् । मस्तिष्कादूर्ध्वं प्रेरयत्यवमानोऽधिशीर्षतः । तद्वा अथर्वणः शिरो देवकोशः समुज्झितः । तत्प्राणोऽभिरक्षति शिरोऽन्तमथो मनः । न च दिवो देवजनेन गुप्ता न चान्तरिक्षाणि न च भूम इमाः । यस्मिन्निदं सर्वमोतप्रोतं तस्मादन्यन्न परं किञ्चनास्ति । न तस्मात्पूर्वं न परं तदस्ति न भूतं नोत भव्यं यदासीत् । सहस्रपादेकमूर्ध्ना व्याप्तं स एवेदमावरीवर्ति भूतम् । अक्षरात् सञ्जायते कालः कालाद्-व्यापक उच्यते । व्यापको हि भगवान् रुद्रो भोगायमानो यदा शेते रुद्रस्तदा संहार्यते प्रजाः । उच्छ्वसिते तमो भवति तमस आपोऽश्वङ्गुल्या मथिते मथितं शिशिरे शिशिरं मथ्यमानं फेनं भवति फेनादण्डं भवत्यण्डाद्-ब्रह्मा भवति ब्रह्मणो वायुः वायोरोङ्कार ओङ्कारात् सावित्री सावित्र्या गायत्री गायत्र्या लोका भवन्ति । अर्चयन्ति तपः सत्यं

मधु क्षरन्ति यद्ध्रुवम् । एतद्धि परमं तपः । आपो ज्योती रसोऽमृतं ब्रह्म भूर्भुवःस्वरों नम इति ॥ ६॥

य इदमथर्वशिरो ब्राह्मणोऽधीते । अश्रोत्रियः श्रोत्रियो भवति । अनुपनीत उपनीतो भवति । सोऽग्निपूतो भवति । स वायुपूतो भवति । स सूर्यपूतो भवति । स सोमपूतो भवति । स सत्यपूतो भवति । स सर्वपूतो भवति । स सर्वैर्-देवैर्ज्ञातो भवति । स सर्वैर्-वेदैरनुध्यातो भवति । स सर्वेषु तीर्थेषु स्नातो भवति । तेन सर्वैः क्रतुभिरिष्टं भवति । गायत्र्याः षष्टिसहस्राणि जप्तानि भवन्ति । इतिहासपुराणानां रुद्राणां शतसहस्राणि जप्तानि भवन्ति । प्रणवानामयुतं जप्तं भवति । स चक्षुषः पङ्क्तिं पुनाति । आसप्तमात् पुरुषयुगान् पुनातीत्याह भगवानथर्वशिरः सकृज्जप्तैव शुचिः स पूतः कर्मण्यो भवति । द्वितीयं जप्त्वा गणाधिपत्यमवाप्नोति । तृतीयं जप्त्वैवमेवानुप्रविशत्यों सत्यमों सत्यमों सत्यम् । इत्यथर्ववेदे शिवाथर्वशीर्षम् ॥ (इति शिर उपनिषत्) ॥

॥ शान्तिपाठः ॥

ॐ सह नाववतु । सह नौ भुनक्तु । सह वीर्यङ्करवावहै ।
तेजस्वि नावधीतमस्तु मा विद्विषावहै ॥

॥ ॐ शान्तिः शान्तिः शान्तिः ॥

(कृष्णयजुर्वेदीय –

ॐ सह नाववतु । सह नौ भुनक्तु । सह वीर्यं करवावहै
। तेजस्वि नावधीतमस्तु मा विद्विषावहै ॥

॥ ॐ शान्तिः शान्तिः शान्तिः ॥)

॥ ॐ ॥

Transliteration

(Transliteration not italicized)

[1]Atharvaśira Upaniṣat (Śivātharva-Śīrṣam)

|| Śānti-Pāṭhaḥ ||

[2]Om bhadraṁ-karṇebhiḥ śṛṇuyāma devā
bhadraṁ paśyemā-kṣabhir-yajatrāḥ |
Sthirai-raṅgais-tuṣṭuvāgun sastanūbhir-
vyaśema hi deva-hitaṁ yadāyuḥ ||

[3]Om svasti na'Indro vṛddha-śravāḥ
svasti naḥ Pūṣā viśva-vedāḥ |
Svasti nastārkṣyo'ariṣṭa-nemiḥ

---

[1] *Atharvaśira Upaniṣat* is also known as *Śira-Upaniṣat*, *Atharva-Śīrṣam*, or *Śivātharva-Śīrṣam*. When it is recited in praise of Lord Śiva (in Śiva worship), it is commonly called *Śivātharva-Śīrṣam*. The Sanskrit text is mainly based on *Āhnika-Sūtra-valiḥ* (see Bibliography).

[2] *Śukla Yajurveda* 25-21

[3] *Śukla Yajurveda* 25-19

svasti no Bṛhaspatir-dadhātu ||

Om saha nāvavatu | Saha nau bhunaktu | Saha vīryaṅ-karavāvahai | Tejasvi nāvadhītamastu mā vidviṣāvahai ||

|| Om Śāntiḥ Śāntiḥ Śāntiḥ ||

([1]Kṛṣṇa-Yajurvedīya –

Om bhadraṁ karṇebhiḥ śṛṇuyāma devāḥ |
Bhadraṁ paśyemā-kṣabhir-yajatrāḥ |
Sthirai-raṅgais-tuṣṭuvāgun sastanūbhiḥ |
Vyaśema deva-hitaṁ yadāyuḥ ||

Om svasti na Indro vṛddha-śravaḥ |
Svasti naḥ Pūṣā viśva-vedāḥ |
Svasti nastārkṣyo ariṣṭa-nemiḥ |
Svasti no Bṛhaspatir-dadhātu ||

Om Saha nāvavatu | Saha nau bhunaktu | Saha vīryaṁ karavāvahai | Tejasvi nāvadhītamastu mā vidviṣāvahai ||

|| Om Śāntiḥ Śāntiḥ Śāntiḥ ||)

---

[1] *Taittirīya-Mantrakośaḥ* (see Bibliography)

Śivātharva-Śīrṣam

Atha Śivātharva-Śīrṣam || (Atha Śira Upaniṣat) || Om devā ha vai svargaloka-māyaṁste rudra-mapṛcchan ko bhavāniti | So'bravīdaha-mekaḥ [1]prathama-māsod-vartāmi ca bhaviṣyāmi ca nānyaḥ kaścin-matto vyatirikta iti | So'ntarā-dantaraṁ prāviśad-diśaś-cāntaraṁ prāviśat so'haṁ nityā-nityo vyaktā-vyakto Brahmā-brahmāhaṁ prāñcaḥ pratyañco'haṁ dakṣiṇāñca udañco'ha-madhaś-cordhvaś-cāhaṁ diśaśca prati-diśaś-cāhaṁ pumāna-pumān striyaś-cāhaṁ Sāvitryahaṁ Gāyatryahaṁ triṣṭub-jagatya-nuṣṭup cā'haṁ chando'haṁ satyo'haṁ gārhapatyo dakṣiṇāgnirāha-vanīyo'haṁ gauraham gauryaha-mṛgahaṁ yajurahaṁ sāmāha-matharvāṅgi-raso'haṁ jyeṣṭho'haṁ śreṣṭho'haṁ variṣṭho'ha-māpo'haṁ tejo'haṁ guhyo'ha-maraṇyo'ha-makṣara-mahaṁ kṣaramahaṁ puṣkara-mahaṁ pavitra-maha-mugrañca [2]baliśca purastāj-jyoti-rityahameva sarvebhyo māmeva sa sarvaḥ [3]samo yo māṁ veda sa devān-veda sarvāṁśca vedān sāṅgānapi brahma brāhmanaiśca gāṁ gobhir-brāhmaṇān brāhmaṇena

[1] Alternative texts: Prathama-māsa vartāmi or Prathama-māsaṁ vartāmi

[2] Alternative text: Bahiśca

[3] Alternative texts: Samāyo or sa māṁ yo

havir-haviṣā āyurāyuṣā satyaṁ satyen dharmeṇa dharmaṁ tarpayāmi svena tejasā | Tato ha vai te devā Rudra-mapṛcchan te devā Rudra-mapaśyan te devā Rudra-madhyāyan te devā ūrdhva-bāhavo Rudraṁ stuvanti ||**1**||

Om yo vai Rudraḥ sa bhagavān yaśca Brahmā tasmai vai namo namaḥ |1||
Yo vai Rudraḥ sa bhagavān yaśca Viṣṇus-tasmai vai namo namaḥ |2||
Yo vai Rudraḥ sa bhagavān yaśca Skandas-tasmai vai namo namaḥ |3||
Yo vai Rudraḥ sa bhagavān yaścendras-tasmai vai namo namaḥ |4||
Yo vai Rudraḥ sa bhagavān yaścāgnis-tasmai vai namo namaḥ |5||

Yo vai Rudraḥ sa bhagavān yaśca Vāyus-tasmai vai namo namaḥ |6||
Yo vai Rudraḥ sa bhagavān yaśca sūryas-tasmai vai namo namaḥ |7||
Yo vai Rudraḥ sa bhagavān yaśca somas-tasmai vai namo namaḥ |8||
Yo vai Rudraḥ sa bhagavān ye cāṣṭau grahās-tasmai vai namo namaḥ |9||

Yo vai Rudraḥ sa bhagavān ye cāṣṭau pratigrahās-tasmai vai namo namaḥ |10||

Yo vai Rudraḥ sa bhagavān yacca bhūs-tasmai vai namo namaḥ |11||
Yo vai Rudraḥ sa bhagavān yacca bhuvas-tasmai vai namo namaḥ |12||
Yo vai Rudraḥ sa bhagavān yacca svas-tasmai vai namo namaḥ |13||
Yo vai Rudraḥ sa bhagavān yacca mahas-tasmai vai namo namaḥ |14||
Yo vai Rudraḥ sa bhagavān yā ca pṛthivī tasmai vai namo namaḥ |15||

Yo vai Rudraḥ sa bhagavān yaccāntarikṣaṁ tasmai vai namo namaḥ |16||
Yo vai Rudraḥ sa bhagavān yā ca dyaus-tasmai vai namo namaḥ |17||
Yo vai Rudraḥ sa bhagavan yāścāpas-tasmai vai namo namaḥ |18||
Yo vai Rudraḥ sa bhagavān yacca tejas-tasmai vai namo namaḥ |19||
Yo vai Rudraḥ sa bhagavān yaśca kālas-tasmai vai namo namaḥ |20||

Yo vai Rudraḥ sa bhagavān yaśca yamas-tasmai vai namo namaḥ |21||

Yo vai Rudraḥ sa bhagavān yaśca mṛtyus-tasmai vai namo namaḥ |22||
Yo vai Rudraḥ sa bhagavān yaccāmṛtaṁ tasmai vai namo namaḥ |23||
Yo vai Rudraḥ sa bhagavān yaccākāśaṁ tasmai vai namo namaḥ |24||
Yo vai Rudraḥ sa bhagavān yacca viśvaṁ tasmai vai namo namaḥ |25||

Yo vai Rudraḥ sa bhagavān yacca sthūlaṁ tasmai vai namo namaḥ |26||
Yo vai Rudraḥ sa bhagavān yacca sūkṣmaṁ tasmai vai namo namaḥ |27||
Yo vai Rudraḥ sa bhagavān yacca śuklaṁ tasmai vai namo namaḥ |28||
Yo vai Rudraḥ sa bhagavān yacca kṛṣṇaṁ tasmai vai namo namaḥ |29||
Yo vai Rudraḥ sa bhagavān yacca kṛtsnaṁ tasmai vai namo namaḥ |30||

Yo vai Rudraḥ sa bhagavān yacca satyaṁ tasmai vai namo namaḥ |31||
Yo vai Rudraḥ sa bhagavān yacca sarvaṁ tasmai vai namo namaḥ |32|| **2**||

Bhūste ādirmadhyaṁ bhuvaste svaste śīrṣaṁ viśvarūpo'si brahmaikastvaṁ dvidhā tridhā vṛddhis-tvaṁ śāntis-tvaṁ puṣṭis-tvaṁ hutama-hutaṁ dattama-dattaṁ sarvama-sarvaṁ viśvama-viśvaṁ kṛtama-kṛtaṁ parama-paraṁ parāyañca tvam | Apāma somama-mṛtā abhūmāganma jyotira-vidāma devān | Kiṁ nūnamasmān kṛṇavadarātiḥ kimu dhūrtira-mṛtaṁ martyasya | Soma-sūrya-purastāt sūkṣmaḥ puruṣaḥ | Sarvaṁ jagaddhitaṁ vā etadakṣaraṁ prājāpatyaṁ saumyaṁ sūkṣmaṁ puruṣaṁ grāhyama-grāhyeṇa bhāvaṁ bhāvena saumyaṁ saumyena sūkṣmaṁ sūkṣmeṇa vāyavyaṁ vāyavyena grasati tasmai mahā-grāsāya vai namo namaḥ | Hṛdisthā devatāḥ sarvā hṛdi prāṇāḥ pratiṣṭhitāḥ | Hṛdi tvamasi yo nityaṁ tisro mātrāḥ parastu saḥ | Tasyot-tarataḥ śiro dakṣiṇataḥ pādau ya uttarataḥ sa oṅkāraḥ ya oṅkāraḥ sa praṇavaḥ yaḥ praṇavaḥ sa sarvavyāpī yaḥ sarvavyāpī so'nantaḥ yo'nantas-tat-tāraṁ yat-tāraṁ tac-chuklaṁ yac-chuklaṁ tat sūkṣmaṁ yat sūkṣmaṁ tad-vaidyutaṁ yad-vaidyutaṁ tat paraṁ Brahma yat paraṁ Brahma sa ekaḥ ya ekaḥ sa Rudraḥ yo Rudraḥ sa Īśānaḥ ya Īśānaḥ sa bhagavān Maheśvaraḥ ||**3**||

Atha kasmā-ducyate Oṅkāraḥ | Yasmā-duccārya-māṇa eva prāṇā-nūrdhva-mut-krāmayati tasmā-ducyate Oṅkāraḥ | Atha kasmā-ducyate praṇavaḥ yasmā-duccāryamāṇa eva Ṛg-Yajuḥ-Sāmā-tharvāṅgi-rasaṁ Brahma brāhmaṇebhyaḥ praṇāmayati nāmayati ca tasmā-ducyate praṇavaḥ | Atha kasmā-ducyate sarvavyāpī yasmā-duccārya-māṇa eva yathā snehena palala-piṇḍamiva śānta-rūpa-motaprota-manuprāpto vyatiṣaktaśca tasmā-ducyate sarvavyāpī | Atha kasmā-ducyate'nantaḥ | Yasmā-duccārya-māṇa eva tiryagūrdhva-madhastāc-cāsyānto nopa-labhyate tasmā-ducyate'nantaḥ | Atha kasmā-ducyate tāraṁ yasmā-duccārya-māṇa eva garbha-janma-vyādhi-jarā-maraṇā-saṁsāra-mahā-bhayāt tārayati trāyate ca tasmā-ducyate tāram | Atha kasmā-ducyate śuklaṁ yasmā-duccārya-māṇa eva klandate klāmayati ca tasmā-ducyate śuklam | Atha kasmā-ducyate sūkṣmaṁ yasmā-duccārya-māṇa eva sūkṣmo bhūtvā śarīrāṇyadhi-tiṣṭhati sarvāṇi cāṅgā-nyabhi-mṛśyati tasmā-ducyate sūkṣmam | Atha kasmā-ducyate vaidyutam | Yasmā-duccārya-māṇa eva vyakte mahati tamasi dyotayati tasmā-ducyate vaidyutam | Atha kasmā-ducyate paraṁ Brahma yasmāt parama-paraṁ parāyaṇañca bṛhad-bṛhatyā-bṛṁhayati tasmā-ducyate paraṁ Brahma | Atha kasmā-ducyate ekaḥ yaḥ sarvān prāṇān saṁbhakṣya saṁ-bhakṣaṇenājaḥ saṁ-sṛjati visṛjati tīrthameke vrajanti tīrthameke dakṣināḥ pratyañca udañcaḥ prāñco'bhi-vrajantyeke teṣāṁ sarveṣāmiha saṅgatiḥ sākaṁ sa [1]eko'-bhūdantaś-carati prajānāṁ tasmā-ducyate ekaḥ | Atha kasmā-ducyate Rudraḥ yasmādṛṣibhir-nānyair-bhaktair-drutamasya rūpa-mupalabhyate tasmā-ducyate Rudraḥ | Atha kasmā-ducyate Īśānaḥ yaḥ sarvān devānīśate īśānībhir-jananībhiśca śaktibhiḥ | Abhitvā śūra no numo dugdhā iva dhenavaḥ | Īśānamsya jagataḥ svardṛśa-mīśāna-mindra tasthuṣa iti tasmā-ducyate Īśānaḥ | Atha kasmā-ducyate bhagavān Maheśvaraḥ yasmād-bhaktān jñānena bhajatyanū-gṛhṇāti ca vācaṁ saṁ-sṛjati visṛjati ca sarvān bhāvān parityajyātma-jñānena yogaiśvaryeṇa mahati mahīyate tasmā-ducyate Bhagavān Maheśvaraḥ | Tadetad-Rudra-Caritam ||**4**||

Eṣo ha devaḥ pradiśo'nu sarvāḥ pūrvo ha jātaḥ sa u garbhe antaḥ | Sa eva jātaḥ sa janiṣyamāṇaḥ pratyaṅ-janās-tiṣṭhati sarvato-mukhaḥ | Eko Rudro na dvitīyāya tasmai ya imānl-lokānīśata īśānībhiḥ | Pratyaṅ-janās-tiṣṭhati sañcukocānta-kāle saṁ-sṛjya viśvā-bhuvanāni goptā | Yo yoniṁ yonimadhi-tiṣṭhatyeko yenedaṁ sarvaṁ vicarati sarvam | Tamīśānaṁ varadaṁ deva-mīḍyaṁ nicāyyemāṁ śānti-matyanta-meti | Kṣamāṁ hitvā hetu-jālasya mūlaṁ buddhyā sañcitaṁ sthāpayitvā tu Rudre |

---

[1] Alternative text: Eko bhūtś-carati

Rudra-mekatva-māhuḥ śāśvataṁ vai purāṇa-miṣamūrjeṇa paśavo'nu-nāmayantaṁ mṛtyu-pāśān | Tade-tenātman-netenārdha-caturthena mātreṇa śāntiṁ saṁ-sṛjati paśu-pāśa-vimokṣaṇam | Yā sā prathamā mātrā Brahma-devatyā raktā varṇena yastāṁ dhyāyate nityaṁ sa gacched-Brahma-padam | Yā sā dvitīyā mātrā Viṣṇu-devatyā kṛṣṇa-varṇena yastāṁ dhyāyate nityaṁ sa gacched-Vaiṣṇavaṁ padam | Yā sā tṛtīyā mātrā Īsāna-devatyā kapilā varṇena yastāṁ dhyāyate nityaṁ sa gacche-daiśānaṁ padam | Yā sārdha-caturthī mātrā sarva-devatyā'-vyaktībhūtā khaṁ vicarati śuddhā sphaṭika-sannibhā varṇena yastāṁ dhyāyate nityaṁ sa gacchet padama-nāmayam | Tade-tadupāsīta munayo vāg-vadanti na tasya grahaṇa-mayaṁ panthā vihita uttareṇa yena devā yānti yena pitaro yena ṛṣayaḥ parama-paraṁ parāyaṇaṁ ceti | Vālāgra-mātraṁ hṛdayasya madhye viśvaṁ devaṁ jātarūpaṁ vareṇyam | Tamātma-sthaṁ ye nu paśyanti dhīrās-teṣāṁ śāntir-bhavati netareṣām | Yasmin krodhaṁ yāñca tṛṣṇāṁ kṣamāñcā-kṣamāṁ hitvā hetu-jālasya mūlam | Buddhyā sañcitaṁ sthāpayitvā tu rudre rudra-mekatva-māhuḥ | Rudro hi śāśvatena vai purāṇeneṣa-mūrjeṇa tapasā niyantāgni-riti bhasma vāyuriti bhasma jalamiti bhasma sthalamiti bhasma vyometi bhasma sarvaṁ ha vā idaṁ bhasma mana etānni cakṣūṁṣi yasmāda-vratamidaṁ pāśupataṁ yad-bhasma nāṅgāni saṁ-spṛśet tasmād-brahma tadetat pāśupataṁ paśupāśa-vimokṣaṇāya ||**5**||

Yo'gnau Rudro yo'psvantarya oṣadhīr-vīrudha āviveśa | Ya imā viśvā bhuvanāni caklpe tasmai Rudrāya namo'stvagnaye | Yo Rudro'gnau yo Rudro'psvantar-yo Rudra oṣadhīr-vīrudha āviveśa | Yo Rudra imā viśvā bhuvanāni caklpe tasmai Rudrāya vai namo namaḥ | Yo Rudro'psu yo Rudra oṣadhīṣu yo Rudro vanaspatiṣu | Yena Rudreṇa jagadūrdhvaṁ dhāritaṁ pṛthivī dvidhā tridhā dharttā dhāritā nāgā ye'ntarikṣe tasmai Rudrāya vai namo namaḥ | Mūrdhāna-masya saṁsevyā-pyatharvā hṛdayañca yat | Mastiṣkā-dūrdhvaṁ prerayatyava-māno'dhi-śīrṣataḥ | Tadvā Atharvaṇaḥ śiro devakośaḥ samuj-jhitaḥ | Tat-prāṇo'bhi-rakṣati śiro'ntamatho manaḥ | Na ca divo deva-janena guptā na cāntarikṣāṇi na ca bhūma imāḥ | Yasmin-nidaṁ sarva-motaprotaṁ tasmā-danyan-na paraṁ kiñcanāsti | Na tasmāt pūrvaṁ na paraṁ tadasti na bhūtaṁ nota bhavyaṁ yadāsīt | Sahasra-pādeka-mūrdhnā vyāptaṁ sa eveda-māvarīvarti bhūtam | Akṣarāt sañjāyate kālaḥ kālād-vyāpaka ucyate | Vyāpako hi bhagavān Rudro bhogāya-māno yadā śete Rudras-tadā saṁ-hāryate prajāḥ | Ucchvasite tamo bhavati tamasa āpo'-śvaṅgulyā mathite mathitaṁ śiśire śiśiraṁ mathya-mānaṁ phenaṁ bhavati phenā-daṇḍaṁ bhavatyaṇḍād-Brahmā bhavati Brahmaṇo vāyuḥ vāyoroṅkāra Oṅkārāt Sāvitrī Sāvitryā Gāyatrī Gāyatryā lokā bhavanti | Arcayanti tapaḥ satyaṁ madhu kṣaranti yad-dhruvam | Etaddhi paramaṁ tapaḥ | Āpo jyotī raso'mṛtaṁ Brahma bhūr-bhuvaḥ svaroṁ nama iti ||**6**||

Ya idama-tharva-śīro brāhmaṇo'dhīte | Aśrotriyaḥ śrotriyo bhavati | Anupanīta upanīto bhavati | So'gni-pūto bhavati | Sa vāyu-pūto bhavati | Sa Sūrya-pūto bhavati | Sa soma-pūto bhavati | Sa satya-pūto bhavati | Sa sarva-pūto bhavati | Sa sarvair-devair-jñāto bhavati | Sa sarvair-vedai-ranudhyāto bhavati | Sa sarveṣu tīrtheṣu snāto bhavati | Tena sarvaiḥ kratubhiriṣṭaṁ bhavati | Gāyatryāḥ ṣaṣṭi-sahasrāṇi japtāni bhavanti | Itihāsa-purāṇānāṁ rudrāṇāṁ śatasahasrāṇi japtāni bhavanti | Praṇavānā-mayutaṁ japtaṁ bhavati | Sa cakṣuṣaḥ paṅktiṁ punāti | Āsaptamāt puruṣa-yugān punātītyāha bhagavā-natharva-śiraḥ sakṛj-japtaiva śuciḥ sa pūtaḥ karmaṇyo bhavati | Dvitīyaṁ japtvā gaṇādhi-patya-mavāpnoti | Tṛtīyaṁ japtvaiva-mevānu-praviśatyoṁ satyamoṁ satyamoṁ satyam | Ityatharva-vede Śivātharva-Śīrṣam || (Iti Śira Upaniṣat)||

|| Śānti-Pāṭhaḥ ||

Om Saha nāvavatu | Saha nau bhunaktu | Saha vīryaṅ-karavā-vahai | Tejasvi nāvadhītamastu mā vidviṣā-vahai ||

|| Om Śāntiḥ Śāntiḥ Śāntiḥ ||

(Kṛṣṇa-Yajurvedīya –

Om Saha nāvavatu | Saha nau bhunaktu | Saha vīryaṁ karavā-vahai | Tejasvi nāvadhītamastu mā vidviṣā-vahai ||

|| Om Śāntiḥ Śāntiḥ Śāntiḥ ||)

|| ॐ ||

APPENDIX A

Significance of the Atharva-Śīrṣas

(The following is the translation of the message sent by Mr. Prem Sharma, which was written in Hindi. The original Hindi text is given after the translation. Mr. Prem Sharma is a retired professional Engineer, who lives in the United States, and is a Vedic and Sanskrit scholar. He has authored many books on the *Sanātana* Dharma and philosophy.)

OM

|| Salutations to Lord Śrī Gaṇeśa ||

A few weeks ago, *Śrī* Vishwambhar sent me a draft copy of his next book (*Atharvaśira Upaniṣat*) for my review. I was delighted. Even living here (in the U.S.A.), in a western world, he has been working hard to serve a divine cause of spreading and propagating the profound knowledge of the Vedas. His efforts are praise-worthy, and he deserves lots of thanks. May he live long; I wish him the best of luck. May God Almighty give him the energy to continue with his excellent work.

During a brief review of the book, I could not resist myself and called him and, as usual, started discussing the Vedic wisdom. *Śrī* Vishwambhar liked my points and asked me to write down my thoughts and give it to him. So, I did.

A Veda is not an ordinary book, or a common holy book describing a procedure for any worship. It is complete knowledge by itself. It is [1]*Vetti,* [2]*Vidyate*, and [3]*Vindate.* The Vedas are referred to as *Veda-Puruṣa*, meaning Veda personified as the Divine Being. A Veda is an ocean of knowledge, which is imperishable, not limited to any time and place; it is for the whole world. It continuously keeps flowing like a river, which has two banks – *Jñāna-kāṇḍa* (part related to spiritual knowledge) and *Karma-kāṇḍa* (part related to Vedic worship). They appear to be two separate banks; however, when the spiritual experience grows and matures, they merge to become one, the way the earth and the sky meet at the horizon. Eventually, they lead to God-realization.

Our great ancient sages and holy thinkers have imparted us these two paths (*Jñāna* and Karma) after deep pondering. We need to perform actions (*Karma-Kāṇḍa*), keeping the spiritual knowledge (*Jñāna- Kāṇḍa*) in mind, and thus, scientifically understand the Vedas in their real sense (and, not to blindly follow the ritualistic part – *Karma-kāṇḍa*). When our actions

---

[1] *Vetti* means 'he knows' – a person who knows *Brahman* knows everything; for him, nothing else is to be known.

[2] *Vidyate* means 'he is' or 'he exists' – a person who knows *Brahman* exists forever because he identifies himself with the *Ātman*, the Inner Self, who is eternal, ever-existing.

[3] *Vindate* means 'he acquires or experiences' – the person who knows *Brahman* has nothing else to acquire since he has already experienced the Truth.

are based on knowledge, we gain more knowledge. We need to intertwine *Jñāna* and Karma since they cannot be separated.

(Each Veda has a *Saṁhitā*, and there are *Brāhmaṇas*, *Āraṇyakas*, and *Upaniṣads*.) The *Upaniṣads* are a medium of acquiring *Jñāna* (spiritual knowledge), whereas, the *Brāhmaṇa* part is a medium to practice Karma (*Karma-Kāṇḍa*). The *Āraṇyakas* help to scientifically understand all. All three – *Upaniṣads*, *Brāhmaṇas*, and *Āraṇyakas* – are different methods to explain the Vedas. They are for learning as well as teaching, performing actions as well as helping others to act, and then finally arrive at a conclusion. The subject of the book is *Upaniṣads*, not the *Brāhmaṇas* and *Āraṇyakas*, and therefore, they will not be discussed.

It is a common practice to call the *Upaniṣads* as Vedānta because they are at the end of the Vedas; this has become an old tradition, perhaps because of the influence of the western Indologists. If we look at them, only *Īśāvāsya Upaniṣad* is the last 40th chapter of the *Śukla Yajurveda Saṁhitā*; no other *Upaniṣad* is "the last part" of any Veda *Saṁhitā*. Of course, the *Upaniṣads* are explained as branches of certain Vedas, but they are not their part. Therefore, it is inappropriate to address them as Vedānta on this basis. The definition of the word Vedānta is, "When, after knowing and understanding it, nothing more needs to be known." That is why the *Brahma-Sūtras* narrated by the Great Sage *Bādarāyaṇa Vyāsa* are called Vedānta; they are the sixth and the last philosophy of *śaḍ-darśana* – six philosophies (*Nyāya*, *Vaiśeṣika*, *Saṅkhya*, Yoga, *Mīmānsā*, and Vedānta).

The *Upaniṣads* could be divided into two categories. In the first category, there are discussions regarding the subtle aspects of *Para-Brahman* (the Ultimate Truth or God-Absolute). These are the dialogues between the ancient sages and their disciples (this category talks about the *Jñāna*, the spiritual knowledge). The second one is the *Upāsanā* category. In the *Upāsanā* category, gradual progress is made – first, by concentrating the mind on an image of a Deity; then, understanding the three aspects of knowledge – (i) *Ādhibhautika* (elemental), (ii) *Ādhidaivika* (celestial), and (iii) *Ādhyātmika* (transcendental). After that, worshipping *Brahman* having a form and attributes (*Saguṇa-Sākāra Brahma*), and finally worshipping and meditating on *Brahman* having no shape and attributes (*Nirguṇa-Nirākāra Brahma*). The second category is simple and appropriate for an ordinary person; The *Atharvaśīrṣas* belong to this category.

The word *Atharvaśīrṣa* is made up of two words – '*Atharva*' and '*Śīrṣa*.' According to *Nirukta* (18-Chapter 11), "*Tharvatiścarati karmā*; *tat pratiṣedhaḥ* – meaning, the *tharva* action is to move, and its opposite is to be steady." Its obvious meaning is to make one 'motionless' who is 'always moving.' In other words, the mind, which is habitually unsteady and wavering, must be made steady and well-focused.

The *Upaniṣads* teach the truth about *Brahman*, who is formless and attribute-less; they remove doubts of the questioner. Initially, for a seeker, it is hard to visualize or understand a formless Reality, which is based on *Jñāna*. Karma is based on *vidhi*, a procedure, which becomes (merely) a tradition (or ritualism) for an ordinary person (if blindly followed, without proper understanding). Our holy thinkers understood this problem, and therefore, after pondering and thinking of the time and limitations, came up with a middle path, which is called *Upāsanā*, (meaning 'to worship and glorify God, and concentrate the mind on His image'). The *Atharvaśīrṣas* are the supporting pillars of the *Upāsanā* method.

Upāsanā begins with concentrating the mind on a Deity having a shape and attributes, and then (with the help of faith, devotion, and dedication, gradually) it turns into the worship of formless and attribute-less *Brahman* – who is very near as well as far. It gives the experience of the extreme Bliss; [1] *Śruti* says, "*Ānandeti Brahma* – the extreme Bliss (experienced within) is *Brahman*."

Upāsanā is founded on faith and devotion (*Bhāva*), and therefore, it is simple, it gives fearlessness. [2]It is like learning the alphabet in school. When we deliberate on the five *Atharvaśīrṣas*, we can quickly learn this secret.

Upāsanā begins by looking at an image (*mūrti*). The celestial beings (gods or devas) are asking Lord Śiva (Śiva. *Atha.* 1.1),

---

[1] Vedas and *Upaniṣads* together are called *Śruti*.

[2] A child learns the alphabet by imagining A for Apple, B for Bat, C for Cat, etc. When he grows, he does not need to imagine these objects to know or use A, B, C, etc. Similarly, a spiritual seeker initially needs an image to concentrate his mind on an object, like an image of his chosen Deity. But, when his spiritual practice matures, he does not require an image anymore, he can easily meditate on *Brahman* or *Ātman*, who has no form and attributes.

"Oh Lord, who are you? …" This question is of a physical or elemental nature (*Ādhibhautika Bhāva*) because the Deity's image can be seen with two physical eyes.

With some practice, when the mind experiences thought vibrations, then, the third eye (*Jñāna-Cakṣu* or the eye of intuition), along with the two physical eyes, experiences the vision of the image of the Deity; this gives birth to the celestial or divine nature (*Ādhidaivika Bhāva*, which is based on the spiritual experience). This is clear from the *Gaṇapati Atharva-Śīrṣa* (*Gaṇa. Atha.*6), "… Oh Lord, You are beyond the [1]three bodies, [2]three states of existence, and the [3]three periods. … etc."

Then, the universal or transcendental nature (*Ādhyātmika Bhāva*) takes birth when the intellect is united with the mind, the thought process is churned, and the duality is eradicated. At this stage, the individual self (microcosm), who has a form and attributes, transforms into the Cosmic Self (macrocosm), who has no form or attributes. Lord Śiva says (Śiva.Atha.1.3), "I am that, I am eternal as well as non-eternal, I am manifest as well as unmanifest, I am *Brahman* as well as the one that is not *Brahman* …" And Goddess *Durgā* says (Devi Atha. 3), "I am personified as the Divine Bliss as well as non-Bliss and knowledge as well as no-knowledge. I am *Brahman*, as well as the one that is not *Brahman* …" This is the concept of all the *Atharva-Śīrṣas*.

---

[1] Three bodies – gross (physical), subtle (mental), and causal.
[2] Three states of existence – waking, dreaming, and deep sleep.
[3] Three periods – past, present, and future.

Here, *Upāsanā* – along with physical (*ādhibhautika*), celestial (*ādhidaivika*), and universal (*ādhyātmika*) natures – submerges in the lake of Blissfulness and gets dissolved; (and the spiritual practitioner, *Sādhaka*, can easily meditate on formless and attribute-less *Brahman*). This is the significance of the *Atharva-Śīrṣas*.

Why are there five *Atharva-Śīrṣas*?

In the creation theory, we are familiar with the term [1]'*Trimūrti*,' but here we are talking about the five *Atharva-Śīrṣas*. It looks like this method of worship is developed to make the journey of life comfortable. In a journey of life – also in an ordinary trip – we need at least five crucial things – the knowledge (*Jñāna*), life, enthusiasm and elation, absence of obstacles, and energy. Lord Śiva grants the knowledge, Lord *Viṣṇu* maintains and reigns life, the Sun-god gives passion, Lord *Gaṇeśa* removes all barriers, and the Goddess – the Mother – bestows energy; who else could be more potent than these? And that is why these five *Atharva-Śīrṣas* – Śiva, *Nārāyaṇa*, Sun-God, *Gaṇeśa*, and Goddess *Durgā* – are an essential part of this system of worship. Each of these Deities is needed for different aspects of life, and therefore, each *Atharva-Śīrṣa* has its own significance.

There is one more critical aspect of the *Atharva-Śīrṣas*; they begin with the same peace chants that make the aspirant

[1] The triad of gods: *Brahmā* – the creator, *Viṣṇu* – the preserver, and Śiva – the destroyer are the three highest manifestations of the one Ultimate Reality, *Brahman*.

selfless and humble. The aspirant, by chanting '*Bhadraṁ karṇebhiḥ* ...,' '*Svasti na Indro* ...' and '*Saha nāvavatu* ...' mantras, desires 'the auspiciousness, the benevolence of all, and cooperation among all, respectively.' Thus, he, with his selfless spiritual practices, very quickly attains the highest divine goal. That is all.

(Original Hindi Text By Prem L. Sharma)

ॐ

|| श्री गणेशाय नमः ||

हमारे कुच्छ हृदयोद्गार

कुच्छ सप्ताह पहले भ्रातृवर्य चि॰ श्री विश्वम्भरलाल ने अपने अगली पुस्तक की ड्राफ्ट कापी हमें भेजी। देखकर अति प्रसन्नता हुई। यहां पर, पश्चिम में रहते हुए भी, सराहनीय कार्य कर रहे हैं, उसके लिये अति धन्यवाद के पात्र हैं – चिरायु हों और परिश्रम कर वेदपुरुष की ऐसी सेवा करते, पश्चिम में इसका प्रसार और प्रचार करें, उसके लिये हमारी शुभकामना !! परब्रहम उन्हें आगे शक्ति दें – यह हमारी प्रार्थना है।

पुस्तक का सिंहावलोकन करते अपने को रोक न पाया, तुरन्त फोन (दूरभाष) उठाया और फिर सदा की भान्ति वार्तालाप आरम्भ हो गया। हमारे कुच्छ विचार चि॰ श्री विश्वम्भर को बहुत अच्छे लगे और हमें उन्हें लिखकर भेजने के लिये आग्रह किया। आजकल मेरा लेखन बहुत शिथिल हो गया है, पर उनका आग्रह, प्रेम और हमारे ऊपर अधिकार और एक ... भाव, इस हृदयोद्गार का कारण बना।

वेद कोई पुस्तक, कोई साधारण ग्रन्थ, या किसी उपासना पद्धति की किताब नहीं है। यह तो स्वयं पूर्ण – वेत्ति, विद्यते, विन्दते – तीनों भावों से भरा **वेदपुरुष** है, जिसका स्वरूप – मूर्ति-दृश्यमान प्रत्यक्ष आकृति है,

उसका भरपूर **ज्ञान सागर** – जो अक्षर है, कालातीत है, सार्वभौम, दिक् देश रहित, और सतत प्रवाहित होता रहता है, बहता रहता है। इस प्रवाह के दो तट हैं – **ज्ञानकाण्ड** और **कर्मकाण्ड**। दिखने में तो ये दो आते हैं, पर जब ज्ञान का सागर आगे आता है तो ये पृथिवी और अनन्त आकाश के मिलन स्थान **क्षितिज** का दृश्य बनकर सामने आ जाते हैं, मानों **वेदपुरुष** का दर्शन हो जाता है, साक्षात्कार हो जाता है। अब ये दो किनारे हमारे लिये, आगे चलने के लिये, हमारे महर्षियों और मनीषियों ने सोचकर हमारे लिये बनाये हैं। ज्ञानसे मनन कर, कर्म करते, **विज्ञानी** बनना है। ज्ञानसे कर्म करना है और कर्म कर ज्ञान प्राप्त करना है, इनको आपस में ताना-बाना समझकर, बो कर (weave), विज्ञान रूप वस्त्र बनाकर, अपने को मलिन वासनाओं से ढकना है, सुरक्षित करना है।

वेद के ज्ञान (काण्ड) के माध्यम हैं **उपनिषद्** और कर्म (काण्ड) के **ब्राह्मण**, और दोनों को मिलाने वाले हैं **आरण्यक** – विज्ञान के दाता। ये तीनों पद्धतियां हैं समझने/समझाने, करने/कराने, और करके निष्कर्श निकालने की। ब्राह्मण और आरण्यक पर लिखना यहां का विषय नहीं है, यहां हमारा विषय उपनिषद् हैं। वेदों के अन्त में हैं तो इनको केवल वेदान्त मानना या कहना एक रूढ़ीगत प्रथा (शायद पश्चिम से) चली आ रही है। देखा जाय तो केवल ईशावास्योपनिषद् ही शुक्ल यजुर्वेद संहिता का अन्तिम चालीसवां अध्याय है, बाकी तो कोई भी उपनिषद् किसी संहिता का "अन्तिम" अध्याय नहीं है। हां, उपनिषद् किसी न किसी वेद की शाखा को लेकर समझाये अवश्य गये हैं, पर अन्त में नहीं हैं। इसलिये इन को केवल वेदान्त कहना हमें युक्ति संगत नहीं लगता। वेदान्त की परिभाषा कुच्छ और है – "जिस को जानने के बाद कुच्छ और जानने या समझने का कोई भी विषय नहीं रह जाय" – वह **वेदान्त**

है। इसलिये ही महर्षि बादरायण व्यास कृत ब्रह्मसूत्रों को, जो षड्दर्शनों के अन्त में हैं, वेदान्त कहा गया है।

उपलब्ध उपनिषदों का सूक्ष्म अवलोकन करने और मनन करने से दो प्रधान तथ्य सामने आ जाते हैं। एक वह है जिस द्वारा केवल परम ब्रह्म की व्याख्या करने के लिये या उन सूक्ष्म तत्त्वों को समझाने के लिये, ऋषियों के वार्तालाप प्रश्न कर्ताओंसे, दिये गये हैं। और दूसरे वो हैं, जिनको उपासना पद्धति से जोड़ कर, ध्यान मूर्ति का वर्णन करते, तीनों – आधिभौतिक, आधिदैविक, आध्यात्मिक – तत्त्वों को समझाते, परमब्रह्म के सगुण स्वरूप का दर्शन कराते, निर्गुण-निराकार उपासना तक पहुचाते हैं। दूसरी पद्धति सर्वसाधारण के लिये अति सुगम हो जाती है – जो ही यहां पर हमारा विषय है। इनको ही **"अथर्वशीर्ष"** के नाम से जाना जाता है।

इस में दो शब्द आते हैं, "अथर्व" और "शीर्ष"। निरुक्त (१८. अ. ११) में आता है – "... थर्वतिश्चरति कर्मा। तत् प्रतिषेधः। – थर्व क्रिया का अर्थ है गति करना, उसका प्रतिषेध है अगति (गतिहीन) करना"। भावार्थ हुआ गतिमान को गतिहीन करना, चञ्चल को अचञ्चल करना – चञ्चल मन को अचञ्चल करे, स्थिर करे।

उपनिषद् निर्गुण-निराकार तथ्य को लेकर शिक्षा देते हैं और उस पद्धति द्वारा प्रश्न कर्ता के शंकाओं-प्रश्नों का निवारण करते हैं। निराकार तथ्य समझना बहुत कठिन है, यह केवल ज्ञान का विषय है, ज्ञानमूल है। कर्म विधि पर निर्भर रहता है, विधिमूल है। जो सर्व साधारण के लिये अवघड़ हो जाता है या रूढ़ी बन जाता है। इन कठिनाइयों को समझकर हमारे मनीषियों ने काफी मनन कर, सोचकर, समय और सीमाओं को ध्यान

में रखते हुए, एक बीच का रास्ता (मध्यम पद्धति) निकालकर दे दिया है जो है "**उपासना**"। और हमारे ये अथर्वशीर्ष (पाञ्चों, जो इस पुस्तक के विषय हैं) इस पद्धति के आधार स्तम्भ हैं।

उपासना, पहले सगुण-साकार को आधार बनाकर, आगे उसका आधार लेते, उस परावर निर्गुण-निराकार में लय कर, आनन्द सरोवर में डुबोकर आनन्द ही आनन्द करा देती है, जिसको ही श्रुति "आनन्देति ब्रह्म" बताती है। उपासना **भावमूल** है, इसलिये भयहीन और अति सरल है। जैसे हम पाठशाला में वर्णाक्षरी सीखते हैं। इन पाञ्च अथर्वशीर्षों पर मनन करेंगे तो यह रहस्य सहज ही सिद्ध हो जाता है। इसका (आराधना/उपासना का) आरम्भ मूर्ति के दर्शन से होता है। देवता शिव से पूच्छते हैं (शि.अथ.१.१), "... रुद्रमपृच्छन् को भवानिति – भगवन्, आप कौन हैं?" यह प्रश्न आधिभौतिक भाव (Elemental Stage) है, क्यों कि यह दो नेत्रों के माध्यम से मूर्ति देखी जाती है। थोड़े अभ्यास से, जब मन पर विचारों का स्पन्दन (Thought Vibrations) शुरू हो जाता है, तो तीसरा नेत्र (ज्ञान चक्षु) इन दो नेत्रों के साथ मिलकर अब इस मूर्ति का दर्शन करता है और आधिदैविक भाव (Celestial Form) का जन्म होता है, जैसे गणपत्यथर्वशीर्ष में (ग.अथ. ६) आता है, "... त्वं देहत्रयातीत:। त्वं अवस्थात्रयातीत:। त्वं कालत्रयातीत:। — भगवन्, आप देह से परे हैं, अवस्था से परे हैं, काल से परे हैं ... आदि आदि"। इस के उपरान्त, चित् बुद्धि से मन को मिलाकर, मन्थन कर, मतिवान होकर, द्वन्दों को डुबाकर, आध्यात्मिक भाव (Universal Being) जन्म लेता है, होता है। यहां पर ही सगुण-साकार व्यष्टि लय को प्राप्त होकर निर्गुण-निराकार समष्टि में मिल जाती है, जैसे शिव कहते हैं (शि.अथ. १.३), "सोऽहं नित्यानित्यो व्याक्ताव्यक्तो ब्रह्माब्रह्माहम् – मैं वो हूं, मैं ही

नित्य हूं तो मैं ही अनित्य हूं, मैं व्यक्त हूं तो मैं ही अव्यक्त हूं, और तो और, मैं ब्रह्म हूं तो मैं ही अब्रह्म भी हूं ..."। और देवी कहती हैं (दे.अथ.३), "अहमानन्दानानन्दौ । अहं विज्ञानाविज्ञाने । अहं ब्रह्माब्रह्मणी वेदितव्ये ... – मैं आनन्द और अनानन्दरूपा हूं, मैं विज्ञान और अविज्ञान रूपा हूं, अवश्य जानने योग्य ब्रह्म और अब्रह्म भी मैं ही हूं ..." । इस प्रकार सभी अथर्वशीर्ष एक ही बात कहते हैं।

यहां पर ही आकर, उपासना उस आनन्द सरोवर में – आधिभौतिक, आधिदैविक और आध्यात्मिक भावों को डुबोकर – लय हो जाती है। यह है इस अथर्वशीर्ष पद्धति का महत्त्व।

पाञ्च प्रधान अथर्वशीर्ष क्यों ?

सृष्टि तथ्य में "त्रिदेववाद" तो आता है पर यहां पर पञ्चदेव अथर्वशीर्षों की क्या उपयोग्यता है, उस पर थोड़ा विचार करें। देखा जाय तो यात्रा को सुखमय करने हेतु ही इस पद्धति का विकास हुआ है। हमें अपनी जीवन यात्रा में कम से कम पांच विभूतियों की आवश्यक्ता होती है (सामान्य यात्रा में भी होती है), और वे हैं – ज्ञान, जीवन, स्फूर्ति, निर्विघ्नता और शक्ति। इन पांचों को समक्ष रखते – भगवान् शिव "ज्ञानदाता", भगवान् नारायण "जीवनदाता और जीवन नियन्ता", भगवान् सूर्य "स्फूर्ति दाता", भगवान् गणपति "विघ्नविनाशक" और महामाया भगवती, मातृ स्वरूपा देवी "शक्तिदाता" – इन से समर्थवान विभूतियां और कौन हो सकती हैं ? इस कारण ये पांच – शिव, नारायण, सूर्य, गणपति और देवी – अथर्वशीर्ष इस पद्धति के प्रधान अङ्ग हैं। हर एक दैव विभूति अपने अपने स्थान और विभिन्न अवस्थाओं और दिशाओं पर आवश्यक है, इसलिये हर एक अथर्वशीर्ष प्रधान है। इस कारण उस

उस अथर्वशीर्ष के देवता (दैव विभूति) को वहां पर प्रधान बताया गया है।

इस पद्धति की एक और विशेषता है कि इन पांचों अथर्वशीर्षों का आरम्भिक शान्ति पाठ उपासक के स्वार्थहीन भाव को दृढ़ करने हेतु है। भद्रं कर्णेभिः ... से "मङ्गलमय भाव", स्वस्ति न इन्द्रो ... से "कल्याणमय भाव" और सह नाववतु ... से "सहयोग भाव" की कांक्षा करते हुए, स्वार्थहीन **साधना** करते, **साधक** अपने **साध्य** को सहज पाता है, पहुंचता है। अलम्।

॥ ॐ ॥

APPENDIX B

Transliteration Guide

Vowels	Trans-literation	Examples
अ	a	like the *u* in h*u*t or *a* in *a*bove
आ	ā	like the *a* in f*a*ther
इ	i	like the *i* in s*i*n or *i*nn
ई	ī	like *ee* in s*ee*n or *e* in *e*ther
उ	u	like the *u* in p*u*t
ऊ	ū	like the *oo* in p*oo*l
ऋ	ṛ	like the *ri* in *ri*d (some pronounce as ru - *u* as in p*u*t)
ॠ	ṝ	like the *ree* in greed (some pronounce as ru, but held twice as long as ṛ)
ऌ	ḷ	like *lri*
ए	e	like the *e* in th*e*y
ऐ	ai	like the *a* in c*a*t or h*a*t
ओ	o	like the *o* in g*o*
औ	au	like the *ow* in h*ow*
ं	ṁ (nasal)	like the *m* in si*m*ple
:	ḥ (aspirate)	final ha-sound *aḥ* is pronounced like *aha* (with a short, stopping sound)

Conso-nants	Trans-literation	Examples
क्	k	as in *k*eep
ख्	kh	as in in*kh*orn or El*kh*art
ग्	g	as in *g*ift
घ्	gh	as in di*g-h*ard
ङ्	ṅ	as in si*ng* or swi*ng*
च्	c	as the *ch* in *ch*eap
छ्	ch	as the *chh* in staun*ch-h*eart or mu*ch-h*arm
ज्	j	as in *j*uice
झ्	jh	as the *dgeh* in he*dgeh*og
ञ्	ñ	as the *n* in hi*n*ge
ट्	ṭ	as in *t*ongue
ठ्	ṭh	as in nu*t-h*ook or an*t-h*ill
ड्	ḍ	as in *d*rum or *d*eath
ढ्	ḍh	as in re*d-h*ot or re*d-h*air
ण्	ṇ	as *n* before d in co*n*dominium
त्	t	as in *t*ube but with tongue against teeth; as *t* in French
थ्	th	as in pa*th* or *th*ought
द्	d	like the *th* in *th*ere
ध्	dh	as in a*dh*esive
न्	n	the *n* in i*n* or as in *n*umber
प्	p	as in *p*erson
फ्	ph	as in *ph*ilosophy
ब्	b	as in *b*eauty
भ्	bh	as in a*bh*or or ru*b-h*ard
म्	m	as in *m*ind
य्	y	as in *y*ellow
र्	r	as in *r*ed
ल्	l	as in *l*ong
व्	v	as in *v*erbal
श्	ś	as in *s*ure

ष्	ṣ	as the *sh* in *sh*ine
स्	s	as in *s*imple
ह्	h	as in *h*umble
क्ष् = क् + ष्	kṣ	*k* and *ṣ* pronounced together
त्र् = त् + र्	tr	*t* and *r* pronounced together
ज्ञ्= ज् + ञ्	jñ	**ज्ञ** pronounced as gya or gña or jña
ऽ	’ (apostrophe)	नमोऽस्तुते = namo’stute (’ is usually silent)

|| ॐ ||

Bibliography

1. 108 Upaniṣad (Jñāna-Kāṇḍa) – Sanskrit-Hindi: By Paṇḍita Śrīrāma Jī Śarmā Ācārya (Saṁskṛti Saṁsthāna, Bareli, India, Revised Edition, 1985)
2. Āhnika-Sūtrāvaliḥ, Śrī-Śukla-Yajurvedīya-Mādhyandina-Vājasaneyinām – Sanskrit: Compiled by Vaidyanārāyaṇa Śarmā; Edited by Vāsudeva Śarmā (Published by Tukārāma Śetye, Printed at NirṇayaSāgara Press, Mumbai, 10th Edition, 1935)
3. Atharvaveda, The – Sanskrit text with English translation: By Devi Chand (Mushshiram Manoharlal Publishers, New Delhi, India, 1997 Edition)
4. Chāndogyopaniṣad: Sānuvāda Śāṅkarabhāṣyasahita – Sanskrit-Hindi: (Gita Press, Gorakhpur, India, 18th Reprint, Hindu Year Vikram Saṁvat 2070)
5. Dancing with Śiva – English: By Satguru Sivaya Subramuniyaswami (Himalayan Academy, India-USA, 4th Edition)
6. Kaṭhopaniṣad – Sanskit-English: By Swāmī Śarvānanda (Sri Ramakrishna Math, Madras, India, 13th Edition, 1981)
7. Liṅga-Purāṇa, The, Volumes I & II – English: Translated by A Board of Scholars; Edited by Prof. J. L. Shastri, Ancient Indian Tradition & Mythology (Motilal Banarasidass Publishers, Delhi, India, 1st Edition, Reprint 1997-98)
8. Liṅga Purāṇam, Śrī-Vyāsa-Maharṣi-proktam – Sanskrit: By Ācārya Jagadīśaśāstrī, Edited by Prof. J. L. Shastri (Motilal Banarasidass Publishers, Delhi, India, 1st Edition, 1980)

9. Mahābhārata Vol. II & VI – Sanskrit-Hindi: Translated by Paṇḍita Rāmanārāyaṇadatta Sāsrtī Pāṇḍeya (Gita Press, Gorakhpur, India, 6th Edition, Hindu Year Vikram Samvat 2051)

10. Mahānārāyaṇopaniṣad – Sanskrit-English: By Swāmī Vimalānanda (Sri Ramakrishna Math, Madras, India, 3rd Impression,1979)

11. Māṇḍūkyopaniṣad – Sanskrit-English: By Swāmī Śarvānanda (Sri Ramakrishna Math, Madras, India, 10th Impression, 1976)

12. Manusmriti, The – Sanskrit-Hindi: Translated by Pandit Girija Prasad Dvivedi (Printed by M. L. Bhargava at Nawal Kishore Vidyalaya, Lucknow, India, 1st Edition, 1917)

13. Matsya Purāṇa, Vol I – Sanskrit-Hindi: (Gita Press, Gorakhpur, India)

14. Muṇḍakopaniṣad – Sanskrit-English: By Swāmī Śarvānanda (Sri Ramakrishna Math, Madras, India, 10th Edition, 1982)

15. Pañcadeva-Atharvaśīrṣa-Saṅgraha – Sanskrit-Hindi: (Gita Press, Gorakhpur, India)

16. Praśnopaniṣad – Sanskrit-English: By Swāmī Śarvānanda (Sri Ramakrishna Math, Madras, India, 7th Impression, 1978)

17. Ṛgveda Saṁhitā – Sanskrit-English (4 Volumes): By H.H. Wilson and Bhāṣya of Sāyaṇācārya, Edited and Revised with exhaustive Introduction and notes by Ravi Prakash Arya and K.L. Joshi (Primal Publications, Delhi, India, 2nd Revised Edition, 2001)

18. Sanskṛit-English Dictionary: By Sir Monier Monier-Williams (Munshiram Manoharlal Publishers, Pvt. Ltd., New Delhi, India, 2nd Reprint 1981)

19. Sanskrit English Dictionary, The Student's: By Vaman Shivram Apte (Motilal Banarasidass Publishers, Delhi, India, Reprint 1979)

20. Sanskrit-English Dictionary: (www.spokensanskrit.org)

21. Śiva MahāPurāṇa, Śrī, Vol. I & II – Sanskrit-Hindi: By Acārya Paṇḍita Śivadatta Miśra Sāstrī (Savitri Thakur Prakashan, Varanasi, India 2000)

22. Skanda Purāṇa Saṅkṣipta (abridged) – Hindi: (Gita Press, Gorakhpur, India, 4th Edition, Hindu Year Vikram Saṁvat 2052)

23. Śrīmad-Bhagavad-Gītā Tattva-Vivecanī – Sanskrit-English: By Jayadayal Goyandka (Gita Press, Gorakhpur, India, 13th Edition, 1996)

24. Śrīmad Bhāgavata Mahā-Purāṇa, Vol I & II – Sanskrit-Hindi: (Gita Press, Gorakhpur, India, 28th Edition, Hindu Year Vikram Saṁvat 2053)

25. Śrīmad Bhāgavatam: In Four Verses – Sanskrit-English: By Vishwambhar (Vishu) Sharma (Printed by CreateSpace, an Amazon.com Company; July 2018)

26. Śvetāśvatara Upaniṣad – Sanskrit-English: By Swāmī Tyāgīśānanda (Sri Ramakrishna Math, Madras, India, 7th Edition)

27. Taittirīya-Mantrakośaḥ, Dvitīyo Bhāgaḥ – Sanskrit: (Sri Ramakrishna Math, Madras, India, 6th Edition)

28. Tattiriya Upanishad, Discourses on – Sanskrit-English: By Swami Chinmayananda (Chinmaya Publications Trust, Madras, India, 1980)

www.ingramcontent.com/pod-product-compliance
Ingram Content Group UK Ltd.
Pitfield, Milton Keynes, MK11 3LW, UK
UKHW021704190726
13853UKWH00001B/410

9 798678 869449